JESUS
TALKED TO ME
TODAY

Books Compiled and Written by James Stuart Bell

JESUS
TALKED TO ME
TODAY

True Stories *of* Children's Encounters
with Angels, Miracles, and God

COMPILED BY

JAMES STUART BELL

BETHANYHOUSE
a division of Baker Publishing Group
Minneapolis, Minnesota

Published by Bethany House Publishers
11400 Hampshire Avenue South
Bloomington, Minnesota 55438
www.bethanyhouse.com

Bethany House Publishers is a division of
Baker Publishing Group, Grand Rapids, Michigan

Printed in the United States of America

Library of Congress Control Number: 2016930776

ISBN: 978-0-7642-1722-7

"An Unexpected Answer" by Ingrid Shelton adapted with permission from "Not a Teacher!" in Therese Marszalek and Sheri Stone, *Miracles Still Happen* (Tulsa: Harrison House, 2003).

"The Pink Vanity Miracle" by Tom Cornelius, as told to Joyce Williams adapted with permission from "A Little Girl's Christmas Prayer" in Joyce Williams, *God Sightings* (Kansas City: Beacon Hill Press, 2009).

Scripture quotations, unless otherwise noted, are from the Holy Bible, New International Version®. NIV®. Copyright © 1973, 1978, 1984, 2011 by Biblica, Inc.™ Used by permission of Zondervan. All rights reserved worldwide. www.zondervan.com

Scripture quotations, marked ESV are from The Holy Bible, English Standard Version® (ESV®), copyright © 2001 by Crossway, a publishing ministry of Good News Publishers. Used by permission. All rights reserved. ESV Text Edition: 2011

Scripture quotations marked KJV are from the King James Version of the Bible.

Scripture quotations marked NKJV are from the New King James Version®. Copyright © 1982 by Thomas Nelson, Inc. Used by permission. All rights reserved.

Scripture quotations marked NLT are from the *Holy Bible*, New Living Translation, copyright © 1996, 2004, 2015 by Tyndale House Foundation. Used by permission of Tyndale House Publishers, Inc., Carol Stream, Illinois 60188. All rights reserved.

The following are true stories, but some details and names have been changed in order to protect privacy.

Editorial services provided by Jeanette Gardner Littleton Publication Services.

Cover design by LOOK Design Studio
Cover photo: Super Stock; Cultura Limited

16 17 18 19 20 21 22   7 6 5 4 3 2 1

To my daughter Brigit Bell Ritchie
in remembrance of the Jesus stories
we read together so many years ago

All grown-ups were once children—although few of them remember it.

—Antoine de Saint-Exupéry, *The Little Prince*

Thanks go to David Horton, Andy McGuire, Ellen Chalifoux, Carissa Maki, Hannah Carpenter, and Stacey Theesfield—you are all so appreciated.

Contents

Contents

Contents

Introduction

Jesus in the Gospels has important things to say about children. He implies that they are the greatest in the kingdom of heaven, their angels continually see the face of God, and it would be better for an adult to drown in the sea than to harm a child.

Though children are born with a sin nature and can be self-centered, it seems that there is also an original innocence they have that displays its own beauty and charm and reminds us indirectly of what we have lost over the years as adults. In effect, Jesus is saying that we should emulate the simple faith, trust, and love that children naturally possess.

As parents and grandparents, we write down their cute sayings and revel in delight at recent videos showing the precious antics of these little ones as they grow bigger. As they become older children, and even teenagers, we marvel at their insights and precocious points of view. There is the temptation to shelter them to avoid the world's moral pollution, and yet we know that they have to face the world as it is and hopefully transform it through their relationship with Jesus.

What may be lost to us, however, in the midst of the birthday parties, soccer matches, and dramatic skits, is the still, small voice of Jesus speaking to us in profound and miraculous ways. Just as He told His disciples not to hinder the children from coming to Him, so we should pay closer attention to our children when they do go to Jesus, seeking His reality in their lives.

Children have a natural affinity for the supernatural. They willingly accept the reality of Jesus because their loving, caring parents tell them He is real, and they can often see Him mirrored in their parents' lives. At times we do not realize the spiritual depth of "Jesus encounters" that our children experience after having accepted Him in literal childlike faith.

And that is what this book is about—experiences of God's supernatural realm from the innocent eyes and ears and hearts of children and teenagers. Enjoy these stories "from the mouths of babes" and be open to hear from the Lord in fresh, sweet, and pristine ways as He enables you, too, to experience Jesus with a more childlike faith than you ever have before.

James Stuart Bell

Like Lava-Hot Electricity

Susan M. Watkins

"You'll need to contact a funeral home."

The words reverberated down the hall, reaching my young ears, then melted around me like the peculiar objects in a Salvador Dali painting.

He's talking about me, I realized.

I stared at the crushed paper beneath my body that failed to cover the surface of the examination table I was lying on.

I heard the words clearly, though they were surreal. They assaulted my ears and shattered my dreams as they hung in the air of the doctor's office.

I was only fifteen years old.

A couple of years earlier, I'd been emotionally drained and disillusioned by my parents' abrupt separation and divorce. The deep wound drove me to find a safety valve to relieve the pressure, and I left home at age fourteen.

A bustling metropolis became my new family. Being hungry was the hardest experience, followed by suffering the brutal cold.

Despite my aimless wanderings, God's steady gaze was fastened securely on me. I was divinely protected. Like Moses backed up against the Red Sea with Pharaoh's army straight ahead, I was positioned for a miracle.

Eventually my circumstances pressed me to evaluate my chosen path, which had turned into a trail of devastation. I longed for simpler times.

I reached the end of myself one year later. Like the prodigal of the Bible, I came to my senses. I returned home, where I was welcomed with feasts of love and sacrifice.

My family members had, one by one, given their lives to our heavenly Father, and shortly after I returned home, I turned to Him, too.

About that same time, I began to feel weary. Considering the lifestyle I'd just left, I assumed I needed to replenish my strength. Yet despite excessive sleep, I remained tired.

Mom took me to our family doctor for a checkup. Sitting in the waiting room, I watched the exotic fish in the elaborate aquarium.

When my doctor examined me, his brow furrowed and his kind expression vanished. Every touch caused excruciating pain and eventual bruising. My mother fidgeted as he drew vials of blood from my emaciated arms.

Everything was double- and triple-checked while he muttered, rapidly taking notes. The nurses became stoic and teary-eyed. I reasoned I must have a bad infection of some kind. I had always been prone to illness and had spent my life battling anemia.

The tension in the room was so thick that Mom nearly broke the handle on her purse. I tried to remain calm. Mom tried to reassure me that nothing was seriously wrong, but this time even she couldn't believe her own words.

After a flurry of activity, Mom rose and went into the doctor's private office, where the walls were lined with Norman Rockwell depictions of physicians holding stethoscopes against young patients. I was left alone in the exam room and strained to hear the distant conversation.

Their voices were grim. I heard my mother weep softly over the muffled words. Then, despite the hushed tones, I heard my death sentence.

He said he'd seen it before, but never this advanced. I was beyond treatment. Nothing could be done for stage 4 cancer, and no therapeutic intervention was possible. His singular advice was to contact an undertaker.

The disease was so aggressive I wasn't even given a life expectancy. I could succumb at any moment.

He called the hospital to arrange tests that would document his diagnosis. A bone marrow specimen wasn't necessary—it would be too painful and not warranted at this final stage.

My mother asked a question too quietly for me to hear. But since the doctor's voice was louder, I could still hear him.

"She won't need a bed. She won't be here that long. We'll give it to someone we can help."

On the short walk home, Mom fought tears and I fought God. I was thin and close to death, but fully prepared to take on the Almighty.

I hadn't yet learned the vital truth about God's love: He is *willing* to be misunderstood by His children during the unknown situations of life.

As brand-new believers, we had no reference point for God's view on terminal disease. My vocabulary was reduced to two words of importance: *God* and *leukemia*.

Within days, I was at the hospital for tests. Barium milkshakes showed internal deterioration. With all my blood nearly drained for testing and my body practically glowing from X-rays, I was virtually sent home to die.

At home, I immediately burst into the Lord's court—but not with thanksgiving in my mouth. I was only fifteen and had dreams and goals.

I swam in my bed of tears, exhausted, and angrily asked, "Is *this* what Christianity is all about? You meet Christ and then you *die*?"

He was quiet in response to my questions. Deafeningly quiet.

My body deteriorated quickly, but I stubbornly lingered. I was on strike. Against death. There had to be an alternative ending.

I could no longer eat, and another month miraculously passed.

Despite my not having any treatment, my long blond hair began falling out. I collected it and threw it away in my bedside trash can, placed there for that purpose. I still frequented the bathroom, because although I could no longer eat, I began to pass internal tissues.

My pain was beyond description, and I grew weaker by the hour. Now with yellow skin, I had no color in my mouth or beneath my eyelids. It appeared that I wasn't going to receive a midnight reprieve.

Confined to bed and feeling terribly alone, I began to smell death on my hands. I've smelled it since then on those near death. It always smells the same. When I tried to scrub the smell away, my yellow hands bled.

My cat also smelled the death spell and refused to come near me. She began her lament and caterwauled nightly at my door. Mom had had enough, and grabbed the hem of God's garment. She wouldn't take no for an answer and decided I would not die before she did. She asked everyone she could how to pray for a healing. Since I was barely alive, *she* became my voice. On earth *and* in heaven.

I was moved to the sofa to be near family since I was no longer able to get up. I remained there wasting away. It was tortuous.

I still had enough focus to pray and fight for my dwindling life. I couldn't understand God's indifference, but made peace with His decision even if it was contrary to mine.

Still longing for health, I placed my failing life into His unseen hands. One last time I prayed out loud, *"Please, Lord, heal me and spare my life. Oh, please God . . . somehow . . . catch me!"*

The pain defied definition but reminded me that I was still alive. Death would end my pain, but it would likewise steal my dreams. I couldn't speak anymore because days earlier I'd lost the ability to take fluids.

I found myself suspended between hope and death, straddling two worlds and incapable of changing the outcome. It is true that dying is hard. Death is the easy part.

With my system rapidly shutting down, I could barely communicate with loved ones. Their questions seemed to take years to reach me, enveloped in multiple echoes. I answered by blinking my eyes. My weight had dropped to eighty pounds, and I was a colorless skeleton. A corpse with a heartbeat.

I, too, grasped Christ's hem and resolved He would either heal me or be forced to drag me around, as I was *not* letting go!

I drifted in and out of consciousness before my heart finally beat its last. I succumbed.

As my spirit separated from my body, I heard my mother's voice sobbing through layers of distant echoes. She'd returned from a Bible study where worshipers explained how to pray for me.

Though I was elated to be free from pain and disease, I paused, realizing I was being given a choice.

I decided to turn back, unable to bear my precious mother's brokenness.

Slowly my spirit returned into a pain-filled body.

I opened my eyes and saw my elated mother, whose words and lips were not synchronized. I strained to comprehend what she was saying.

She explained what she'd learned and announced that we would pray for my healing. We did, but nothing happened.

Perplexed, we tried again. Nothing.

Mom regrouped and prayed again. I just stared at her—it was all I could manage. Again, nothing.

Suddenly she asked, "Do *you* believe the Lord can heal you?"

I heard myself saying it but couldn't release the words. Finally, with a weak, parched voice, I managed to verbalize, "I belie—."

It was as far as I got, when suddenly the heavens bowed low, the Lord came down, and I felt His enormous right hand gently cradle the top of my head.

No words can describe the power that was released into my being. A type of almost lava-hot electricity that neither burned nor injured entered my body from His hand.

My head was touched first to record these events. The thick, hot power traveled slowly. Slower than molasses in winter, but steady and consistent. Nothing could deter its mission.

Every part this power touched was instantaneously healed. When it reached my shoulders, it branched out in synchronized precision and traveled down both arms at the exact same rate of speed. Upon exiting my fingertips, the power at my collarbone resumed its downward journey.

I became immediately aware of my physical body. Knowing exactly how things looked internally, I could have drawn detailed illustrations. For as God's gentle power permeated my body, I became acutely aware of my own intricate design.

His healing balm continued. I longed for it to reach my stomach—my area of greatest pain—for everywhere God's power touched, I was dramatically healed. Conversely, where it had yet to reach, I was still dying.

Finally reaching my abdomen, it divided and moved in unison down both legs. I lay there unable to move under God's power and felt as if I were actually luminous.

I finally spoke, declaring, "I'm healed!"

We were frozen in that divine moment, hushed and awestruck by God's holy presence.

Exiting that agonizing journey taught me deep lessons about God's unwavering faithfulness and unfathomable love.

At the tender age of fifteen, I was lavishly chosen to experience firsthand a demonstration of the Lord's overwhelming involvement in His children's lives and His inextinguishable desire to release His healing power. I was privileged to share in the sufferings of Christ and to declare the pristine nature of our Good Shepherd—who still leaves the ninety-nine to rescue the one caught beneath life's fence.

With His single touch, my terminal disease recoiled. He alone stilled my storm with one command. It will take all of eternity to thank Him.

Giants in the Land

Wanda J. Burnside

I loved going to school. While Daddy worked at Cadillac Motors in Detroit, Michigan, Mama stayed home taking care of the three children: Rodger, my brother; Regina, our baby sister; and me.

At ten, I was the oldest. Rodger was nine, and Regina was seven. We went to the same elementary school in our neighborhood. The families who lived around us cared about one another. One day that assumption changed.

As Rodger, Regina, and I walked home from school together, three big boys started to pick on us.

"Hey!" yelled a tall boy. "Do you have some candy, gum, or money?"

"You better give me some, too!" said another boy, shaking his fist.

"You ain't gonna make it past us!" shouted a really big boy with one of his front teeth missing. He giggled and his tummy shook.

I grabbed Rodger and Regina's hands and we ran home.

The next day after school, the same boys were there to taunt us again.

"Hey! Where's my bubble gum?" one boy shouted.

"Give me some money so I can buy some chips!" yelled another.

Surprisingly, my science teacher, Miss Kelly, drove by very slowly. She followed us in her brown-and-yellow station wagon. We made it home while the boys looked on.

"I'm tellin' Mommy!" said Regina.

"They aren't going to do nothin'! I'll knock them out!" Rodger said with his fists balled up and standing like a boxer. "I know one of those boys. Nobody is scared of them!"

We went into the house, and Mama was in the kitchen fixing dinner. She welcomed us home with a quick kiss.

"How was school? Go wash your hands and get ready for your snack," Mama said.

I went upstairs to the bathroom to wash my hands. On the wall in the hallway hung a very large picture of two children, a boy and girl, walking across a scary-looking wooden bridge that hung by truly dangerous old ropes. Several planks on the bridge were broken; others were missing.

Under the bridge, waves splashed high in the river. Near the children was a giant-sized angel with large wings. She watched the children as they walked across the rickety bridge at night.

That picture had hung in our hallway for years. But that day it seemed especially beautiful . . . and comforting. I kept staring at it.

When I came downstairs, Mama asked me to help set the dinner table. She looked puzzled and said, "What's on your mind?"

"Mama, you know that big picture in the hallway upstairs? Is that a fairy godmother watching those children on the bridge?" I asked.

"No, that's an angel watching over the children," she said. "The angel watches so that nothing bad will happen to them."

"I wish I had an angel like that watching over me. She could take care of Rodger and Regina, too. Nobody could bother us then!" I said.

"Why do you say that?" Mama asked. "Is someone bothering you? Tell me."

Mama's face was very serious. She was not smiling.

"Three boys!" shouted Regina. "Every day when we come home from school, they try to bother us. But we run home."

"I don't like the sound of that. Wanda, I want you to talk to your dad about this when he comes home tonight," Mama said, putting the plates on the table.

After dinner, we sat in the living room and told our parents what was happening on the way home from school. Dad said that we shouldn't have to be afraid of anyone. He said he would go to the school and speak to the principal about it.

Then Dad read from the Bible about how the Lord is with us and will protect us. He said God would send His angels to camp around us. He said there were trillions of angels, more than enough to help us. Then Dad and Mama prayed for us.

Rodger, Regina, and I felt much better after telling our parents about the boys. We were tired of them. I wished they would just go away.

Rodger and Regina did not go to school the next day, so I walked home with some of my girlfriends. I didn't see the boys, and I was happy about that.

One of my friends, Pamela, wanted us to go to a store with her to buy some candy. When we came out of the store, the boys were waiting for us. They grabbed Pamela's bag of candies. They laughed and stuck out their tongues as they ran away.

Pamela cried, and so did the other girls.

I was mad. I wondered, *Where are the angels?*

That weekend, I was happy that we were going to be with our grandmother and our young uncles who lived with her. We always had lots of fun with them.

On Friday night, Uncle Fred turned off the TV and spent time talking and playing with us. Then, just before bedtime, he asked us if we had studied our Sunday school lesson. We said yes, but he loved to test us to see if we knew it.

He read it to us first, but he read the wrong lesson. We told him it was not the lesson for this Sunday. He checked it, and we were right. He had read the lesson for the next month.

However, the lesson he read was about how God's angels helped His people.

Rodger, Regina, and I were so excited. We told Uncle Fred that this was what Dad and Mama had been talking to us about.

"God didn't make a mistake," he said. "I reckon you needed to hear that lesson tonight."

Then we told Uncle Fred about the three bad boys near our school. He laid his hands on our heads and prayed for us. He asked God to help us every day and to send His angels to be with us. We felt extra special after that.

When we walked to school on Monday, we felt brave. We didn't feel afraid coming home from school, either. We laughed and skipped around as we walked. Then we ran and couldn't stop giggling. We made it home safely.

"No big boys!" we told Mama as soon as we came home. She was so happy.

At dinner we told Dad, and he smiled. Then he told us that he'd reported the boys to the principal. In a way we were happy, but we were also a bit sad because we didn't want those boys getting back at us because they'd been reported.

The next day and the rest of the week, we didn't see the boys. It was wonderful. We didn't feel afraid anymore. All the children in the neighborhood were happy. They played tag, baseball, and basketball. They rode their bikes and jumped rope.

Then one day I had to walk to the store to get some bread and milk for dinner. As I was going down the aisle to get the bread, I saw one of the boys. My heart leaped and I felt sick in my stomach.

He looked at me, balled up his fist, and then went to the counter to pay for a box of cereal.

I was so afraid; I waited for him to leave. Then I went up to pay for our food. The man bagged the bread and milk and handed them to me with a smile. I ran out the door, and then looked around, but did not see the boy.

I walked to the corner, and then walked across the street to the other side. I still did not see the boy or any of the others. My heart was beating like a drum.

"Hey! Girl! Where are my treats? Where is my . . . Wow! Oh! Wow!" he said with terror written on his face. His eyes were so big! His mouth opened wide and he screamed, "Look at that man! He's a giant!"

The boy ran.

I didn't understand. I looked around. I was afraid. *Where is the giant the boy was talking about?*

I didn't see him. But I didn't care who the boy saw. He was gone. Good!

The next day after school, I was walking home with Regina. Rodger had joined the baseball team and had stayed behind. Regina was singing a song about angels: "All night, all day, angels watching over me, my Lord."

Regina sang it again. She said she'd learned it in school that day. I caught on and began to sing, too.

Then the three boys jumped out with several more . . . there were eight or ten at least. They stood in front of us.

"Where's that big man?" asked one boy.

"I saw him the other day with her!" said the boy who'd been in the store that day.

Then the boys said, "Aw! There ain't no man . . . Uh?"

They looked up and yelled, "Who is that? Wow! Look! Giants!"

"Look at them! There's fire around them! Look!" shouted another boy.

"They're taller than a tree! As tall as that apartment building!"

"Come on! They've got swords!" another boy cried.

And then all of the boys ran off.

Regina and I just stood there and looked. The boys kept running until we couldn't see them anymore. Regina and I wondered what had happened.

Then I stopped right on the street and looked up into the sky. I saw a bright light shining. I felt warm and calm. I did not feel afraid.

Regina sang her song again. We held hands and smiled.

"Angels!" Regina said. "Angels!"

"Yes, Regina," I replied, "God sent His mighty angels to protect us."

We ran home and told Mama what had happened.

"The Lord is with you!" she said.

The next day, Rodger joined us on our way home from school. The angels were there, too. Children gathered, looking at us. After that day, girls and boys in large groups walked around us, wanting to see those big men who chased the boys away from us.

For the next month they followed us. Some of the children said they could see them, too. This made them ask us about our angels. We told them about how our parents and Uncle Fred had prayed for us to be protected.

We became known as "the children with giant angels around them." We never saw those boys again. From time to time there were some challenges in the neighborhood, but God continued to be with us and watch over us.

We were tremendously blessed by the Lord for the rest of our days—from elementary school through to college—while we lived in the same inner-city neighborhood. One thing is for sure: We learned to trust God and to believe His Word. We never doubted God because He'd sent us angels to prove He was watching out for us.

We Never Have to Say Good-bye

Trish Propson

"God gave me the words to a song, Mom!" my ten-year-old daughter, Jenna, said as she burst into the room.

"That's nice, dear," I replied wearily.

In the days after September 11, 2001, everyone seemed emotionally exhausted and unsure of even the most basic things. I did not have the strength to join my daughter's childish declaration of faith. But she persisted. For weeks after the attacks she pursued me, passionately describing how God was speaking to her directly about the emergency rescue workers who had died in the towers.

I dismissed her repeatedly.

"Pray about it. Write down what God is telling you," I suggested.

"Mom, please sit down and listen to me," she begged three weeks later.

I slumped into a chair. In the background the television flashed tragic images of failed rescue attempts at the pile of rubble now called Ground Zero. I listened halfheartedly as she began to read what she had written.

"God told me to write a song about the rescue workers who died in the towers. Their children didn't get to say good-bye to them and they are very sad. God has a message for them." She spoke with a confidence and passion I had not noticed before.

As she read the words to the song God had given to her, my heart came to life. I knew the words my young daughter spoke could not have been created by her child's mind. The words were filled with deep mourning and unspeakable pain.

I listened as she recited profound words of restorative hope and healing. When she finished, I sat awestruck. I realized she had indeed heard from God.

I looked at the horrific images on the TV screen and back to the innocent trust in my daughter's eyes.

"What does God want you to do with the words to the song?" I finally asked, wiping away a sudden flood of tears.

"Oh, that? Simple. He asked me to write the song, make a CD, and go to New York to give it to all the children who lost a parent." She spoke with a transparent faith and determination that only comes from an encounter with God. She skipped off excitedly to play outside.

I watched her through the window as she danced through the fall leaves with her younger siblings.

"What do you want from us, God?" I prayed.

Trust her.

New thoughts blazed through my mind as I pondered what could happen next.

For the next thirteen months, we worked on "the song." As Jenna shared her vision with musicians and church leaders, the simple lyrics from God's heart to my child took on a life of their own. We were quickly swept into a new world of song writing, sheet music, recording studios, musicians, voice talent, artwork, and copyrights. Dozens of professionals rallied around her vision. She never doubted that she'd heard from God and never wavered in her commitment to fulfill God's command regarding the song.

My doubt constantly interrupted the process. Her goals seemed impossible. But Jenna kept saying, "Mom, if God wants it to happen, He will show us what to do. We just have to listen to what He is telling us."

We prayed about the song every day. Our entire family was immersed in the project. When we hit roadblocks, she often came back with a God-sized solution. In her faithful heart, everything seemed reasonable.

God asked her to put all the names of the fallen rescue workers on the CD jacket so that every child's parent would be listed. We found that no official list existed and controversy surrounded the names of the deceased rescue workers. When I was ready to give up, she exclaimed, "God says to make the list for the CD cover ourselves, Mom."

Trust her. God's words rang in my heart.

After months of research and contact with the officials in New York, we had an approved list to print on the CD cover.

"See, I told you!" she exclaimed.

Walking through a local bookstore that spring, Jenna stopped at a painting of a firefighter with an American flag. The print was titled *No Greater Love*. We studied it for a few minutes before moving on.

A few days later, she came to me. "Remember that painting at the bookstore, Mom? God says that should be on the cover of the CD."

"We can't just use it on the cover. The painting is copyrighted. Painters don't just give away the rights to print their work," I reasoned.

"Well, this one will," she announced.

A professional musician and songwriter helped Jenna finalize the lyrics. She suggested the title change from "We Never Got to Say Good-bye" to "'Cause We Never Have to Say Good-bye."

This simple shift in lyrics brought a new level of eternal hope for grieving families who would see their loved ones again in heaven. The change was brilliant and made sense to everyone involved in the song project. Jenna declared, "I will have to ask God if that is what He wants us to do."

And so it went for the rest of 2001 and into 2002. We moved forward with the project. I coordinated all of the details. Jenna prayed and shared God's directives as He gave them to her. God edited and approved the final lyrics. When we needed a recording studio, God provided. Professional studio musicians and digital sound mixing artists embraced the vision and volunteered.

Contact with government organizations and 9-11 families seemed effortless. A donation for discs and reproduction came from an unknown source. Approval and digital artwork from artist Ron DiCianni for the CD cover came as my daughter had predicted. Money for printing was donated and friends packaged the CDs, complete with a bow and a prayer for each of the children who would receive the song.

Jenna's faith faltered briefly in early September 2002. She thought all along that God wanted the CD distributed at the first-anniversary ceremony commemorating the brutal World Trade Center attacks. When all doors seemed to close and the anniversary date came and went, she questioned if any of what she had heard was real. When she doubted, God gave me the strength and resolve to encourage her.

The CD was finished and shipped to a 9-11 family organization shortly before Thanksgiving. We prayed over the plain brown shipping cartons and watched as what began as a directive from God moved down a sterile conveyor belt toward an unknown future. It seemed anticlimactic. I sighed in relief, assuming we had completed the task God had given my daughter thirteen long months before.

She was unsettled about the CD. Thinking she was just grieving the end of the project, I tried to comfort her.

"I just think there is more to it, Mom," Jenna said. I looked into the eyes of a young girl who had matured far beyond her years because of "the song."

"I trust you," I said.

The organization in New York received the CD shipment and called two weeks before Christmas, asking her to come and sing for the fallen rescue workers' children at a Christmas party later that week. I declined, knowing I could not afford or arrange a trip to New York City in four days.

"Oh, did I forget to tell you?" Jenna asked with an innocent smile. "God said we are going to New York, and He will pay for the trip and make all the arrangements."

In her mind it was already done. I shook my head in amazement and called the person back to say we would be there. The next day, a man donated frequent-flyer miles. A transit strike in the city left all hotels in Manhattan overbooked. A couple from church offered a pre-booked hotel room just a few miles from where Jenna was to sing.

Trust her. God whispered again into my doubting mother's heart.

We spent a week in New York singing her song, meeting with 9-11 families, touring police and fire stations, and visiting Ground Zero. God met every need during the trip—from free limousine transportation in the gridlocked city to personal contact with government officials and seats on a wait-listed flight, my daughter prayed, never doubting that God would swiftly answer.

God used the song to change Jenna. She has never questioned her trust in Him, even during her turbulent teen years. She often reminded me that God chose her to serve Him once and she trusted that He would continue to guide her steps.

God used my daughter's unwavering commitment to His guidance to strengthen my own faith. Many times as trials threatened to overtake me, I was reminded to trust God even when things seemed impossible.

God used the words of my daughter's song to impact the hurting families of the rescue workers who lost their lives attempting to save others. He used the simple faith of an obedient child to bring hope and healing to thousands of children who lost a parent in the Twin Towers on 9-11.

Many years later, Jenna still stays in contact with the people she met during that journey. Now a police officer herself, she would tell you that she heard directly from God when she was just ten years old, and the words to that song changed everything.

The Heavenly Messengers

Diane M. Nunley

One of my first assignments in my nursing career was on a community hospital pediatric ward. There I learned how children behave during illness and trauma.

It's hard to watch children die. They maintain their love of life and desire to play almost to the end. Their fears focus on the immediate concerns: a needle stick, separation from their parents during a test, or being isolated from other children during their illness.

Rarely has a young child asked me if death is imminent or inquired about an afterlife if he or she has not been taught about eternal life.

During this time I also learned about how parents suffer with their afflicted children. So when my five-year-old cousin was diagnosed with ALL, acute lymphocytic leukemia, I knew I would learn a new dimension of suffering through the hearts of my mom's sister and her young daughter, Kimberly.

Kimmy's illness lasted over an eighteen-month period with the usual prolonged hospital stays, blood transfusions, drugs, and the tears of our entire family.

Not only was I a young new nurse, but I was also a new Christian. I felt convicted to discuss eternal things with my aunt, but her grief and the angst of watching her daughter suffer kept her from hearing my verbal witness. I decided my best approach was to love her and my cousin through action.

The disease progressed, and my desire to explain a simple version of eternity to my small cousin increased. However, the opportunity never seemed to arise. I visited Kimberly often, praying for her and her mother through each visit.

Finally, about a week before Kimberly's death, I was able to visit her alone at the children's hospital. Most of the children on her ward were also cancer patients, and many were in isolation rooms. Each time they entered an isolation room, families and staff had to "dress out," donning paper gowns, masks, hats, and gloves. These were a precaution so germs wouldn't be transmitted to an immunosuppressed patient, but the isolation garb easily disguised the identity of the visitor.

One day when I entered the room I called out, "Hi, Kimmy. How's it going, honey?"

I approached her bed and grabbed her frail little hand with my gloved fingers as I reached under her oxygen tent.

"Is that you, Di?" She turned her pale face toward me, the dark sunken circles glaring beneath her tired young eyes.

"It's me . . . how's your bunny?" She clutched to her chest a worn stuffed rabbit with floppy ears. We had spoken through the bunny before—the bunny had tests or pain, frequently riding to the X-ray department or laboratory. She was always "good."

The drone of the misted oxygen persisted as Kimberly blinked her eyes. She raised the toy just slightly above her chest.

"He's awful tired today," she said, dropping the rabbit to the bed.

"Aw. I'm so sorry to hear that. What are we going to do?" I smiled as I noticed the small brightly patterned suitcase at the foot of her bed. "What's this? Are you going somewhere?"

"Pretty soon. They told me to pack and get ready." She strained to raise her head and look at the suitcase.

"Over there," she said motioning toward the window and dropping her head back down. "They've been here two days."

If I had been talking to a child raised in church, I would not have been surprised that she was thinking about heavenly messengers. Most church education programs teach Bible stories early. But since Kimberly had never been to church, I was intrigued to discover the identity of the visitors at my cousin's window.

I have found that most children have deep faith in the adults around them. They assume they will be fed and cared for. Kimberly was no different; she never expressed fear through her words or actions during her illness. Her precious little smile prevailed as her lips became bluish from severe anemia. To my knowledge, she had never received teaching about angels or a biblical heaven; therefore, her allusion to supernatural visitors was stunning.

"I will have lots of toys and other kids to play with," she said, her eyes brightening. Then her countenance changed.

"What's wrong, honey?"

"I can't take Bunny . . . but they said I can leave him behind to make another sick kid happy. I guess it will be okay." She clutched the toy closer.

"Where are you going with them?"

"Home. They are taking me home. A new house. And Mama can come, too!"

"Who are they, Kimmy? Did they tell you their names?"

"Friends. I think they were angels. I have my stuff packed in the suitcase Grandma gave me," she said.

I continued to question her about their dress, voice, hair color and style. Did they come into the room or stay at the window? Was their appearance only at night, or did they also come during the day? Were they men or women?

Her answers were quick, to the point, and her demeanor remained peaceful and assured. I learned the angels were boys and girls that looked like the teens down the street from her home, and they had appeared for several nights in a row outside her window.

She'd packed her suitcase with the help of a night nurse and insisted it be kept at the foot of her bed.

"Are they here now?" I asked.

I had heard confessions from patients who talked about seeing loved ones or heavenly messengers a few days before death, so I didn't want to discount her testimony. Besides, how could she have made up such a story when she had no previous training about God's messengers?

"Not now. They came again this morning and said they would be back tonight. I've already told Mama to get ready, too. Will you make sure Bunny goes to a new kid?"

"Certainly I will. You just tuck him under the covers when you go, and he will fall asleep until I get here. Okay?"

She nodded, clutched the rabbit to her chest, and closed her eyes. She had lost so much weight that her little eyes bulged out under her half-closed lids.

I said good-bye and knew I had to talk with my aunt. I believed Kimmy's death to be imminent.

My aunt was resting in the waiting area, cigarette smoke clouding her weary face. "Did she tell you about the angels?"

"Yes. She did. I think it will be soon."

She snuffed out her cigarette, stabbing it into the ashtray with fierce strokes. "I guess I should call the priest."

"Do you have one?"

"Don't look at me like that. I know I should. I know I should have taken her to church long ago. It's too late now—"

"Not too late for Kimmy. Seems like she's ready for heaven. She expects you to be there, too." Not the most brilliant theological introduction . . . but it opened the door.

"Why don't we check with the hospital chaplain? Someone will come and visit with you, I'm sure."

I thought the loss of her daughter might open her heart to hear the gospel, but more realistically, I feared the anger and bitterness would shout over God's extended grace. The hospital chaplain made his visit after I left for the day.

Within the week Kimmy passed away and was buried. The day after her funeral, I returned to work on my pediatric unit, but never completed my shift.

I was on duty only an hour before I collapsed. I was taken to the emergency room, where my doctor diagnosed a ruptured ovarian cyst. I would need surgery to stop the internal bleeding.

As I waited for my operation, a young doctor dressed in greens and a lab coat visited me. He patted my hand, winked, and nodded as if to say, "You'll be fine."

I felt assured but didn't recognize him. It was July; all the new interns and residents were beginning their rotations. I didn't think too much about not recognizing him until I pressed the nurses to identify my visitor.

"No one was in here," my colleague explained. "I've been right outside your room and am sure you had no visitors."

Kimmy's heavenly messengers had appeared to her as familiar neighborhood teens. Was it possible my visitor was also a heavenly messenger? I took comfort in knowing that just as God had sent His angels to reassure my cousin, He had sent a heavenly messenger my way, too.

My young cousin's faith and acceptance of the news of her impending trip with her new friends strengthened me in my hour of need.

Forty years later, after studying and teaching the Bible, I have gained knowledge and understanding I did not have back then. Yet I still wonder on that night if one of heaven's newest arrivals, a five-year-old little girl with a suitcase, intervened on my behalf to request a messenger to bring me comfort in my time of need.

Jesus Outside the Window

Heather Spiva

A sudden and pitiful cry woke me from my sound sleep. *Oh no. Another nightmare!*

My youngest son had always slept soundly—until he turned two years old. I rolled over, hoping he would go back to sleep.

He howled again—more intensely this time. Apparently we weren't going back to sleep any time soon. Not tonight.

I grabbed my robe and walked to my son's room. As I opened the door, I heard him whimper.

I sat on the edge of his bed and we went through the ritual of comfort, talking, prayer, and more comfort.

Sometimes the comfort—just hugging and holding him— would help. At other times, I'd need to return to his room a couple of times to get him calmed down enough to go back to sleep.

I whispered to my son, "Caleb, Jesus loves you very much. Any time you have a bad dream, pray to Him. Tell Him you are scared. Pray that He will take the scary part away. He is always here for you and with you, even when you don't see Him."

We had repeated those words often in our house. In fact, we had used them initially for my oldest son, Joshua, who had gone through a similar phase of bad dreams a few years earlier. We would say them to him after we prayed and before we closed the door. It was a necessary ritual. He needed to hear it to feel safe. We needed to say it because when he felt safe, we could sleep!

Their fear and bad dreams seemed to come from a variety of things—perhaps seeing things they shouldn't have seen on TV, an especially overwhelming day, or just a normal childhood bad dream.

And so I prayed and said the comforting words Caleb needed to hear on this particularly cold night. Though I'd said the same words a hundred times, it was just one more time—one more time for my boy who was sad and scared and needed comfort.

After that night of bad dreams, a long string of nights passed quietly, and the nightmares seemed to be a thing of the past. I didn't think too much about it. I was just glad he wasn't waking us in the middle of the night with his terrified cries.

One evening my husband and I were in Caleb's room, praying our bedtime prayers together. Afterward, it was my turn to tuck him in, say the right words, and make sure his teddy bear and beloved blanket were close by.

I turned out the light and walked back to sit on the edge of his bed. I repeated the words I said every night.

Caleb listened as usual. He nodded and stuck his thumb in his mouth, his blanket tucked under his nose. I sang his favorite song to him and leaned in for a kiss.

When I got up to leave, I noticed Caleb's pensive attitude but chalked it up to his being tired. As I was about to close the door, he said, "I saw Jesus last night."

I stopped dead in my tracks.

"You saw who?"

"Jesus." Caleb pointed to the window, the blinds closed and curtains drawn.

I was well aware that my two-and-a-half-year-old boy was just that—two and a half years old. And he was a child with an active, if not overactive, imagination. Hence the reason for the bad dreams, and the reason for the prayers, and . . . perhaps the reason he told me he had seen Jesus.

I walked back to his bed and sat down slowly. "So, you saw Jesus, huh?"

"Yup. He was here."

"Okay," I nodded, my head racing. *I can't believe he got to see Jesus!* I wanted to yell and scream and jump up and down. *How amazing is this? Jesus?*

But I didn't want to lose the moment. I didn't want to lose the truth my child was telling me—that he had seen the most important person in creation. The One who did everything for us. The One who loves us unconditionally . . . so much so that he came to my little boy's room to show him that He loved him. He cared about his sleep; He cared that he hurt.

It wasn't logical. It was miraculous.

"So, was He in the corner?" I asked, trying to visualize where He would have been.

"No. I saw Him in front of the window. He was right there," Caleb said, pointing to a dark wall.

I nodded again. I didn't know what to say.

"That is so wonderful. That is the best thing that could've happened, honey."

Such lame words for such a fantastic event!

Caleb looked at me. He smiled.

"It sure is. And I'm not scared now."

I was trying desperately not to cry. That would've confused my sweet boy. So I wiped my eyes and said, "What a great thing He has done for you."

I kissed Caleb again, looked once more at the darkened area where the window was, and closed the door behind me.

I practically ran to the kitchen to find my husband and tell him the good news.

The good news of Jesus. The news that gives us peace and everlasting life . . . and a good night's sleep.

God answers prayers in His own way and in His own timing, and for good reason. My son seeing Jesus' face as the answer to our prayers was worth all the times I'd gotten up in the night. It was truly a great thing.

Indeed, what a great thing He did and continues to do for us.

Wonders in the Night Room

Suzelle Johnston

Born with a clubfoot and a slightly flattened palate, the child arrived a little too early on a day when the parents didn't expect. But that didn't matter because these parents felt any time their child chose to come was a very welcome time.

This baby was wanted from before the pregnancy. Girl or boy, they didn't know and they didn't care. They chose names for him or her, and they waited, impatient for their first introduction.

They'd already waited for a child for more than ten years. And when he or she was finally conceived, what joy they knew! God was so good.

Like Hannah of the Old Testament, who'd prayed for a son, or Elizabeth of the New Testament, who when it was hardly possible found herself celebrating the birth of her son, this mother-to-be gave thanks that her prayers were finally answered.

Not even the warning of possible issues dimmed the couple's joy. So what if the father's blood type was O-positive and the mother's A-negative. Was that a problem? They didn't know. The doctors, however, understood the risk and were concerned.

Even though the baby was premature, that was okay, because their daughter was born with a fringe of red hair and blue eyes and the right number of toes and fingers. And if her heart was a little damaged, the doctors hoped she'd eventually outgrow it.

"Of course she will," her parents insisted. "Don't you know? God answers prayer."

The young mom overheard the words *congenital heart defect.* She didn't fully understand the words, but whatever they meant, these new parents would simply pray. Because here in their arms was all the proof in the world that God answers prayer.

After some time in the hospital, the baby was allowed to go home. No one was surprised by the joy in that house. This child's parents had only enough money to scrape by, but they showered their little girl with a waterfall of love. And they felt rich in the wealth of their love.

Then small things started happening—sickness, unexplained fevers, more sickness. Their baby girl just couldn't seem to get well.

Of course, at that time medicine wasn't as advanced as it is now, and the doctors didn't know how to fix some of the problems. The clubfoot wouldn't straighten, no matter how it was wrapped. But surgery helped. And so did two years of corrective shoes.

The flattened palate? The doctors did nothing because, after all, the little girl loved to laugh and sing. Maybe she spoke with a lisp and couldn't learn the difference between left and right.

But she did learn to pray. Wasn't God that gentle shepherd in a long robe who carried a lamb in His arms? Like in the picture on her wall?

He also loved big-eyed bunnies, ponies, and all children everywhere. But of course, baby girls were probably his favorite, her mother said.

The perfect imperfect little girl managed to charm everyone who cared for her. One young doctor cared so much that he wrote his home number on a card.

"Call me if you need anything," he told the worried mother. "I'll come."

And he did. In the middle of the night, when another fever stayed too high. Or to a quiet room with news no one wanted to hear.

The little girl had so much energy. Was she really that sick? Did she have to stay so quiet?

It was a vicious circle for the mother, knowing if her child played and ran like other children, her fever would spike and that damaged heart would flail and stutter.

A church full of prayers rose as a vigil was held. Those who wanted to believe in a God of miracles gathered to pray. They called upon a God who once whispered, "Peace! Be still."

They remembered that He knew what it was to be tossed back and forth upon a sea where nothing looked safe. And maybe He *was* the only one on that small ship who wasn't afraid, but He also understood His companions' fear. He knew how fragile people could be, that storms of fear and worry could swamp the faith of even the strongest.

Yet even in the storm, in all the rage and rain, He spoke so few words. He looked into the sea burning and boiling in its fury. And He simply whispered, "Peace."

Isn't that what we all want to hear when fear and doubt wake us in the middle of the night, storming in our hearts and wringing out what faith we somehow try to cling to?

These parents, this church, and the doctors who stood at the girl's side wanted to believe He whispered still.

"Peace."

But the storm continued. Rheumatic fever. Heart murmurs. A heart able to sustain less and less activity. Worst of all for that mother was another whisper she wasn't supposed to hear: "She won't live past the age of sixteen."

And that was only if, somehow, this child managed to live to the age of six.

Peace?

Where was such grace to be found?

Certainly not in the years of hospital visits that followed. There were so many different hospitals with long corridors and longer needles. The little girl learned the drill: Another blood test. Another examination. Another hospital room where she would be left alone.

But she wasn't really alone. The music of the angels and the stars and the heavens sang to her.

She never told anyone about the angels coming to her room at night—how they would sing and laugh and smile. But when the stars spun circles in the sky, when she was alone and the lights were turned off, the room would glow and she would listen.

Music, beautiful music, beautiful dreams, songs of the spirit that only a child's heart could hear. A great choir sang anthems of praise. Pictures of a glowing world she'd never seen filled her mind with beauty and gave her the feeling that she, who'd always had to be careful, at last had the freedom to run and play. And all the while, there was the music.

Rainbow-colored streams, magical forests where trees towered and touched the sky. Laughter and butterflies and birds with shining wings stretched so wide. She would have said it was like the stories her mother told, fairy tales of a princess in a castle. The beauty and the fun she had . . . princess or child sweating out a fever from another bout of pneumonia or something else, there in her dreams, in the darkness of a hospital room. Listening to the music.

So much light and love filled her room that she'd smile and wait. She knew *He* would come. In all the light and sound, His was the face she looked for.

Sometimes He was one of the singers; sometimes He led the choir. Sometimes He just listened. But then He'd smile at her like He knew some great secret—as if He had so much more to share.

She recognized the look in His eyes. He looked at her with the same expression as the man in the picture on her wall at home. He looked as though the lamb in His arms was precious and dear to Him.

She wasn't afraid when she looked into His eyes. He loved to sing and laugh—with her, with the others, and the stars—in the light. And when she became too tired to play, He'd sit at the foot of her bed and tell her it was okay to go to sleep. She figured He meant she'd wake to see another morning.

And she did. Every night she listened and dreamed.

And healed.

The rheumatic fever lasted almost three years. The heart that shouldn't have been strong didn't stop. During all that time, it didn't weaken.

Instead, it survived.

It beat steadily and sure, and she was allowed to go home.

It clipped along when she walked, pounded strong when she ran. What was once a feeble, hesitant heart became sturdy and strong.

This puzzled her doctors.

"Why?" they wanted to know.

Because God answers prayer.

Because He spoke the word: "Peace."

And maybe her failing, struggling heart heard that word, felt the power of it, and even as the waves of a storm had calmed once before, her heart rested at His command.

Only He knows for sure. But for those two parents, it was a miracle.

And what of the child?

She lived.

She lives still. The memory of the music hasn't dimmed. At times she thinks if she listens hard enough, she might hear as once she did with the ears of a child: the songs the angels sing at midnight when the stars spin circles and darkness is filled with light.

Holy Laughter

Jeanne M. Phelan

I sat alone at the long table in the orphanage cafeteria and stared at my bowl of oatmeal. I picked up my spoon, but a wave of nausea swept over me.

Jimmy! Where is Jimmy?

Feeling hopeless at the thought of facing life without my older brother, I put my spoon down.

Suddenly I was startled by a blinding light. I turned and stared into the face of a young man clothed in radiant white and seated next to me.

My heart pounded in terror as I scooted away from him to get off the bench and kneel before him.

"Don't be afraid."

Tenderly, the angel comforted me and told me God sent him to tell me I wasn't alone because God is my Father in heaven. This glorious man said he was an angel and told me not to bow before him, because we are to worship only God.

Then he added, "Jimmy is okay, Jeanne. You don't have to worry."

"Jimmy! God knows about Jimmy?"

The angel assured me that God knows everything. He promised to stay with me to help me eat my oatmeal. He told me God was healing me.

As he spoke, warmth filled my tummy, pushing the nausea away. I grabbed my spoon and devoured the hot, creamy oatmeal. I scraped the bottom of the bowl and wanted more.

The angel smiled and waited as I ran to the kitchen, where the nuns happily filled my bowl. The angel grinned at me through the serving window.

The nuns were delighted to see I was still hungry. They knew about my problem with keeping my food down and my weight loss. This was my first day out of the infirmary since my arrival at the girls' home. The nuns had prayed for me to be healed, and though they weren't aware of the angel, these kind, joyful women knew their prayers had been answered.

Born in St. Paul, Minnesota, in 1944, to a large Irish family, I entered the revolving door of foster care as a toddler, paired with my big brother Jimmy, who was two years older than I was.

My battle with anorexia began in our last foster home the day I received a tricycle with red and white streamers on the handlebars. Excited, I waited all day for Jimmy to come home and see me ride it.

I never rode the trike. I learned at dinner that Jimmy had been sent to an orphanage without me. I choked and gagged on my food. The tight, hard ball that had pressed down on my tummy all afternoon shot up with a vengeance. The contents of my stomach hurled into my hands and seeped through my fingers, the rotten smell staining the white tablecloth.

Because of repeated nausea and vomiting, I was no longer allowed to eat at the gracious dining room table. Next we tried my meals in the bedroom, then in the basement stairwell. But all the hot meals served by my foster mother were eaten and promptly thrown up.

I managed to keep down snacks and sandwiches at kindergarten. And my foster mother took me to the doctor due to weight loss. She wanted him to give me "a good talking to."

The elderly doctor asked her to step outside. He said he was a Christian, and God's love washed over me as he comforted me and cradled me in his arms. He said my eating problems stemmed from my sorrow over losing Jimmy and promised to pray for my healing.

Healing! The doctor's and nuns' prayers were finally answered as God sent my new heavenly friend!

When I returned from the kitchen, the angel smiled and asked me to tell him what I knew about Jesus. I told him about baby Jesus being born and sang a few verses from "The Friendly Beasts," a traditional Christmas song that talked about animals bringing gifts to Jesus.

He enjoyed my singing. I told him other facts about Jesus dying and rising from the dead. But mostly I told him about Santa and the reindeer and the Easter Bunny. I finished by saying I preferred Christmas to Easter because I didn't like jelly beans.

I can still see his hands moving in front of him as he took my jumbled facts and swept them off the table. He said in a firm voice that he didn't want to talk about Christmas or Easter anymore. He wanted to talk about the cross. Now that was something I was sure I had straight.

"The Roman soldiers nailed Jesus to the cross. They killed Him."

The angel looked at me silently like he was waiting for something. I tried again and told him the mean soldiers were to blame.

"Jesus died for your sins!" he said, as his eyes locked with mine.

How could that be? I thought. *I didn't have anything to do with it. It was a long time ago and I wasn't even born then!*

His eyes penetrated the depths of my heart and soul. I knew that I was known, nowhere to hide. My sin caused Jesus to die on the cross. The Roman soldiers had my help.

As I continued to gaze into his eyes, I saw a scene that had happened in my foster mother's home before I'd been sent to the orphanage. One day she had broken down, cried, and begged me to forgive her for her harsh treatment of us.

I had asked if I could see Jimmy again.

When she said no, my heart snapped shut.

"I hate you!" I had screamed, stamping my feet. "I hate you and I will never forgive you as long as I live!"

Now as I sat with the angel, I felt ashamed of myself.

I hung my head. I wanted another chance with her. Was it too late for me to tell my foster mother I forgave her?

I begged the angel to find her for me. He said he went only where God sent him but assured me God would take care of her.

"But remember," he told me, "all through your life it will be very important for you to forgive others. And about that heart of stone . . ."

I jerked up my head. *He knows about that?*

Months earlier I'd prayed to have a heart of stone so that I would never feel hurt again. Now I knew God had been listening when I'd uttered that prayer.

"Jesus can take that heart of stone," the angel explained.

I prayed anew. I bowed my head and asked God to forgive me and to please give me a new heart. And I invited Jesus to live in that new heart.

Cleansing tears fell. A huge burden lifted from my shoulders. Jesus now lived inside me and I would live with Him forever in heaven.

I looked at my bowl of oatmeal. Almost gone.

The angel and I watched the nuns clean the nearby tables—they were still unaware of his light that flooded the room with glory.

"Why can't they see you or hear you?" I asked.

"Why should they?" he asked.

I told him they were religious, which meant they were holy. At the word *holy*, the shining angel lost his dignity. Laughter bubbled up. He threw his head back and let out a loud belly laugh; he held his stomach and laughed and laughed. The musical sound bounced off the walls, filling the room with melody, and wrapped me in unspeakable joy.

I joined in, feeling as if I were being tickled all over. In my mind, I saw a picture of angels and God's children before the throne being tickled, and I saw how much delight God the Father takes in all of us who belong to Him.

As the angel and I continued to talk, the angel's long, tapered fingers fascinated me. When he spoke, he waved his hands as if he were conducting music. His skin was translucent, and the radiance that beamed from him lit the darkest corners of the old cafeteria. He looked like he could be a member of my family, with blue eyes and light brown hair that fell to his shoulders. I leaned back on the bench to examine the angel's back.

"How did you get here? You're supposed to have wings!"

We burst out laughing again. As I swallowed my last spoonful of oatmeal, the angel disappeared.

I didn't say anything to the sisters about the angel. Instead, I ran outside to play. Love for Jesus burned in my heart, and I started to talk over everything with God. I missed Jimmy but wasn't afraid to live without him. I longed for a family of my own.

Three years later I received my heart's desire: a visit to Jimmy and adoption!

I kept silent about the angel for forty years. But through the years of marriage and raising children and helping with grandchildren, I've learned to settle my accounts quickly. That was the lesson I learned as a five-year-old the day the angel came to help me eat my oatmeal—the day God set me free to forgive!

Thanks to God's ministering to me through His angel, I've learned the truth of Colossians 3:13: "Bear with each other and forgive one another if any of you has a grievance against someone. Forgive as the Lord forgave you."

A Man in a White Dress

Bev Gattis

It was a sad naptime for two-year-old Jason. At lunch, Daddy, always silent and moody, had ignored his son's questions and had simply walked away.

Jason had wanted to know why he couldn't see Jesus, why we talked to God and He "didn't talk back," and where heaven was.

The questions from the small boy were complicated, and his daddy didn't have the answers, so instead of trying to respond, he walked away without a word.

Our son came to me with huge tears in his eyes. "Why Daddy not talk? Why Daddy not know 'bout Jesus?"

I could only assure him that his father loved him even if he didn't answer his questions. I made sure he understood that Daddy did know about Jesus; he just didn't know how to provide an answer that would inform and comfort his son.

I could not disappoint the toddler who naturally adored his father, so I simply held him close and whispered, "It's okay. Daddy is tired right now, little man."

Hugs temporarily soothed Jason, but he couldn't forget his father walking away from him. With his naptime pacifier in place, he soon ended his soft sobs and drifted into a deep sleep.

Two hours later, a little longer than his usual nap, I heard a tiny voice talking as if in response to a waking dream, or perhaps it was the simple musings or songs this creative child was known for. I waited for his call, but this time he came out of his bedroom himself with a look of wonder on his face.

"Mama, he told me something."

Aware that his daddy was not in the house during his nap, I knew my son must have been talking about a dream. This was not unusual for him.

I said, "What, son? Who talked to you?"

He looked at me accusingly, like he thought I should know. He frowned and, with all the patience a two-year-old could muster, he said firmly, "Him standing by my window. I waked up and he said, 'Jason Earl, Jesus loves you!'"

Tears gathered in my eyes as my small son insisted that "a man in a white dress" sat by his window as he awakened, then spoke his name. Never particularly shy, Jason said he stared at the man who had a big smile as he told him that the Lord Jesus loved him "bestest."

It was far more comfort than a silent daddy or a frustrated mama could have given. I spent the next several weeks feeling deep, grateful humility that God would send an angel to speak peace to my two-year-old.

Jason talked about this incident again and again—to a silent daddy, who nodded and accepted that it happened, and to a surprised grandma and grandpa who didn't know how to react, since church was never part of their schedule. Yet they understood that their grandson was not making up stories—it was certainly a real memory for him.

Shortly after that, an angel appeared again. Jason went into the kitchen late at night to retrieve his ball that had rolled there. The kitchen was dark, but when Jason turned back to the living room, he stopped and stared at the doorway. He seemed a little afraid to come out of the darkened kitchen.

"Mama! Please come get me! That man in the doorway is too big," he said with a whimper.

I had been painting a ceramic project, so I looked quickly and saw nothing, but laid down my paintbrush. Before I could get up from the chair, my son suddenly walked out of the kitchen and turned around to face the doorway. A huge smile crossed the boy's face as he nodded to the visitor I could not see.

"He says it's okay. He gone now; I not scared," Jason said.

I wondered about the incident for a long time and finally concluded that the angel appeared to my child so that in his little mind he would consider the hugeness to be a powerful and awesome protection.

A full year later, as I held Jason and his eight-month-old brother on my lap to read a favorite storybook, he suddenly pointed, "Look, Mama! That man is outside our window now."

I was surprised, for I had thought the angel forgotten. I really wanted to see what my son was seeing, so I looked hard to catch a brief movement or quick glimpse of what an angel looked like.

"There! By the bush!" Jason insisted

I asked him to tell me what he was seeing. Now three, he was a little frustrated with me, but said firmly, "Mama, he's on a white horse. He got a white dress and a big sword. He 'members me; he smiled again!"

I saw nothing outside the window by the bush but told my son that he was seeing his angel who kept him safe at all times. Of course, this led to further questions. I tried to make sure he understood that sometimes we can see our angels and sometimes we can't. But God loves us so much that He has His angels watching over us all through our lives.

I was amazed that my son was allowed to see into the spiritual world in this way. It helped him cope with a silent earthly father who truly loved him but simply did not know how to deal with a child's questions.

Jason never again mentioned an occasion where he saw his protective angel. But his awareness of God's love grew steadily.

He grew up to become a wise, patient, creative, and loving husband first, then father to a young daughter and son. He never doubted God's great love for him and was always certain of God's abiding presence in his life.

That certainty was highlighted recently when his own toddler stepped off the dock and sank into the deep, dark waters of the lake where they vacationed. At twenty-two months, Mason didn't understand that the lake water was not safe to walk on.

Daddy Jason ran, jumped in, and caught the precious red-haired boy. Instant praise rose in Jason for that long-term protection and love of a holy heavenly Father who continually showed himself awesome. When he told the story later, he said, "I can only praise my Savior for His constant provision and protection in my life."

The adult Jason doesn't remember the visits by his protective angel. He loved to hear about them as he grew, but recalls little of those special moments. But the firm conviction of God's love and protection has never been anything less than vivid and comforting to him.

One day little Mason will be told that he, too, is loved by the earthly daddy God gave him as well as our Father in heaven who protects like no one else can, just as Jason as a toddler was assured by his mama and a special angel who appeared to him that he is one of God's "bestest."

Pulling Our Heartstrings From Heaven

Lisa Plowman Dolensky

"Mommy, Mommy, wake up!"

I was sound asleep when my five-year-old son, Max, crawled into my bed shouting. Even though I was blurry-eyed, I could tell his little face was pale and worried.

"Mommy, I had a dream. I was up in heaven."

"Really?" He needed no prompting to keep talking. In fact, Max was talking so fast and animatedly that he reminded me of a sped-up chipmunk cartoon. And I was trying my best to decipher and hold on to his every word.

"There was an angel. It told me to tell you that I had this dream. But I couldn't tell if it was a boy angel or a girl angel. The angel showed me trees where you could just wish for what you wanted to eat and the food would be there like magic. There were even candy trees. I also saw children angels learning to fly. It made me laugh when they fell down trying."

"Well, could you fly with your wings?" I asked.

"No, because I was just there visiting. They don't want me there yet," he said.

I was relieved and smiled at his excitement.

Then his whole body started shaking, so I pulled him close in my arms.

"Then I saw this really long, shiny train. It had a gold and silver shiny engine with a face on it with sparkly blue eyes and gold-rimmed glasses. The face talked and said she was Grandma Herdman. She had a really nice laugh."

How sweet. Max has maybe heard us speak of Grandma Herdman, I thought as I recalled his father's grandmother. I also thought it was cute because Max loves to play with toy trains more than anything.

Max spoke even faster, a bit like a chugging little locomotive himself. I felt his heart pounding through his pajamas, beating as if to keep up with the pace of his speech. His forehead began to sweat as it was pressed to mine. Then he looked at me hard in the eyes without blinking.

"The funny thing was she only carried tires in her train. Hundreds. Too many to count. I've never seen a real train, TV train, or pretend one in books carrying tires.

"Mommy, you won't believe what she told me. . . ." He gulped and whispered with watery eyes, "She said, 'I have a warning for you, Max. Stay out of the street today, because you might get hit by a red car.'

"Mommy, she said it over and over. She knew my name. She knew that I loved to play with trains. I felt like I knew her, too, and I wasn't afraid of her."

My smile faltered a bit as I thought about this. Grandma Herdman had passed away two years ago, before Max was old enough to remember his great-grandmother. Just now when Max had mentioned that the train cars in his dream were full of tires, I instantly knew his unusual dream had to be a message from heaven. Grandma Herdman had retired decades earlier from a B.F. Goodrich tire plant in Akron, Ohio. This was something that Max wouldn't know.

During Grandma's last weeks of life, she had told me she had been hit by a Model-T Ford on a dirt road at the age of five and had to learn to walk again. More facts Max wouldn't be aware of. Max also had a favorite battery-operated remote control car that he loved to play with nearly every day outside on our driveway beside our sometimes-busy street. A feeling of eeriness and peace washed over me simultaneously.

I kissed Max's forehead and assured him that his dream was God's way of telling him that his angels were watching over him.

I told him that his sweet Great-Grandma Herdman had loved him very much. I also told him that I believed his dream was a message from her to be careful so he would be safe.

I explained that when she was on this earth, she had worked at a place that made thousands of tires, and that's why she carried tires in her train. I encouraged him to pay attention to his dreams, and that heaven was real and something to believe in.

"So were the tires where she worked too many for me to count?" His eyes widened as he asked the question.

"Yes, too many for you to count," I said.

The last time Max had seen Grandma Herdman alive he had been about three years old and had begged to carry his toy doctor's kit to the hospital when we visited her. He walked in the door announcing, "I'm here to fix you!"

"Oh, I see," she said with a smile as she spied the toy doctor's kit in his hands.

Max played doctor, listened to her heart, and gave multiple pretend shots to make everything all better while she softly laughed. She smiled as he used the toy reflex tool like a hammer to supposedly adjust her bed as she secretly moved the controls. He thought he was really moving her bed.

"It's magic," he muttered as he banged away. She chuckled and called him "Magic Max."

"Thank you, Dr. Max. I'm feeling so much better," she told him as she winked at me. "My bed even feels better. I'm ready to go home now." Then she pointed up to the ceiling.

I wondered, *Does she mean go home to heaven?* But I didn't ask.

When I was alone with her, Grandma Herdman told me she had lost her mother as a young child, before she herself was hit by the car. She thought her accident erased the memories she should have had of her mother.

"I could never remember anything that happened before the accident," she told me. "I just had to believe what people told me about her, and they would sometimes say my mother was looking down from heaven at me."

Grandma died a few weeks later. And now she had found a way to communicate with her great-grandson, who had been too young to remember her alive. But I knew without a doubt she had remembered their last visit and was looking down at us from heaven.

When Max and I went outside, the weather was beautiful. But I heeded Grandma Herdman's safety warning. We usually played on the driveway first during the cool part of our summer mornings, but instead, on this day, we chose the backyard.

Later I placed family photos on the coffee table without saying a word to Max, as he pushed his wooden trains and configured tracks all around it. When he noticed the random photos, he picked up the photo of Grandma Herdman and said, "Mommy, look! This is Grandma Herdman—the talking face I saw on the train. She's so cool! She went to heaven and gets to pull tires."

Then he went right back to playing. I was once again thankful for how she had pulled at our heartstrings all the way from heaven.

In the Palm of His Hand

Elissa M. Schauer

My nearly four-year-old son occupied his usual perch that Friday morning. Kneeling on a chair at the kitchen table, he focused on the paper and crayons before him. His artistic bent during that season seemed slightly cathartic. So whenever I stepped into the kitchen, he accompanied me, working ploddingly on his numerous masterpieces. Even though he occasionally chatted about whatever thought flitted through his mind, his eyes never left his paper.

But that Friday morning was anything but usual. A phone call had come late the night before. *Collapse. Paramedics. Airlift. Hospital. Surgery.* The panic in my father-in-law's voice on the other end of the line had filled the room, choking out a response. My husband and I sat in stunned silence until the second phone call an hour later. The surgeon had used the word *grave* speaking of my mother-in-law's condition.

My husband's flight left before dawn, so while he flew from Boston to Phoenix, I was alone that morning with our son. Fatigued by the long, sleepless hours, I wondered how to explain something so difficult to a child about his sweet grandma—the gentle and fun woman who had sat at that very table with him only two weeks before, laughing and coloring. The grandma whose motto was "Always say yes!"

"Grandma, let's go for a walk!"

"*Yes!*"

"Grandma, play catch with me!"

"*Sure!*"

"Grandma, here's a fun game for us to play!"

"*You betcha!*"

"Grandma, will you read that again?"

"*I'd love to!*"

Over and over. Again and again. She never tired of anything and everything with her grandchildren. Where repetition overwhelmed even the heartiest of parents, Grandma stepped in with her nearly supernatural endurance. Her smile and that contagious giggle were a resounding *yes*.

So this morning I sat next to my little one and waited for the right moment to catch his gaze, when there was a pause in his activity to hold his attention. I then attempted to explain what had happened and where Daddy was, using truthful terms my son could comprehend without frightening him. His only question affirmed that he indeed understood.

"Will Grandma die?"

I wanted to reassure him, *No! Most certainly not!*

I wanted the neurosurgeon to be wrong. I wanted to tell my tenderhearted little boy that there would be more birthdays and Christmases, more trips to the zoo and swings on the swing. I wanted there to be more time, and I desperately wanted to be able to deliver such words of comfort to him.

But I couldn't lie to him. His earnestness required the truth.

"I don't know."

He returned to his creative task of crayon to paper, and I turned away. No longer able to hold back the tears, I looked out the window over my sink. I was overwhelmed by all that had transpired in less than twelve hours, and I was anxious at the thought of what was ahead of us in the next few days.

Then after a few minutes of attempting a morning routine, there came another question.

"Momma?"

He didn't look at me, still concentrating on his work while he thoughtfully reflected. I turned and watched him as he paused, wishing so desperately that I could prevent the reality of this day from ever touching his world.

But the wheels were turning in his mind. His art was merely sensory integration—a venue for him to do some of his best thinking. So I feared what other truth I might need to reveal with his next query.

As his right hand continued the busy back-and-forth strokes of a crayon, his left hand reached out with an upturned palm, cupped as if catching raindrops. But instead of asking a question, he posed a statement. Instead of seeking my knowledge, my little boy offered wisdom as he stared at his outstretched hand.

"Momma, maybe God will hold Grandma in the palm of His hand."

Out of the mouth of my babe came this prophetic utterance of hope. Only the divine can reveal this kind of hope. He was not parroting a phrase he had heard from us, so I knew the genuineness of its source. I held my breath, knowing my kitchen had become holy ground.

After he spoke, his eyes moved from his cupped hand to me, and then returned to his artwork. He was back to being nearly four.

As the hours became days, we experienced the fulfillment of those words. God held my mother-in-law in the palm of His hand through two delicate brain surgeries to repair that blood vessel that appeared to have been sliced open. And despite what the doctors had initially told us—that her brain scan was that of a dead person—she returned to us and eventually to her home.

During the three-month stay in the hospital, my father-in-law teased the neurosurgeon that he and God were doing a great job. But even a medical expert couldn't take credit for what had transpired, so the surgeon held his hands two inches apart and said, "I've done this much." Then he spread his arms wide and continued, "God has done this much."

We had six more years together, and although the complications from the aneurysm meant that grandchildren played puzzles and games with Grandma instead of fishing and riding bikes, there were still more birthdays and Christmases, and enough laughter to fill a lifetime.

After her memorial service, my son reflected on how good it was to just sit and talk with Grandma—that they didn't really need to *do* anything because it was just so good to *be* together. And I thought of him as a four-year-old in the kitchen of our old house, communicating a dependence on God that was far beyond what he had experienced or could know.

I knew that God had indeed held Grandma in the palm of His hand—at that moment, over the next six years, and during every day of her life.

God's Waiting Room

Kendy Pearson

"It hurts." Rachel shifted in the truck seat.

"Here, take my hand." Rachel's mom helped her scoot across the seat. "You're probably just stiff from the long ride."

Rachel grimaced as she jumped to the ground. She stumbled over the rest-area curb and hobbled to the restroom. She felt ninety years old instead of nine. Too soon, the family was on the road again. They had yet to reach the halfway point between the campground in Canada and their home in Oregon.

Darkness shrouded the truck cab as it lumbered into the driveway, rocked by the sway of the camper. Rachel rubbed the sleep from her eyes and started to slide across the seat to the door. A bone-deep twinge caused her to whimper as her mom helped her to the ground. Thoughts of her Little Mermaid sheets made her smile. After ten days of sleeping in a sleeping bag, she couldn't snuggle into her soft bed soon enough. Tomorrow she could ride her pony again and see if the duck eggs had hatched.

Bright rays of gold warmed the room the next morning as Rachel stretched and her eyes traced the winding green vines of the wallpaper.

Ugh, Monday. One week closer to the end of summer vacation, she thought.

As she did every morning, Rachel tossed her Ariel sheet aside to swing her feet to the floor. Unlike every morning, however, heaviness filled her hip bones and stabs of pain accompanied each movement. Her steps slow, she wandered into the kitchen to see who was up.

Tuesday morning brought even more discomfort for Rachel, so her mom called the doctor.

Rachel sat with a *Highlights for Children* magazine spread open on her lap.

Are they ever going to call my name?

The fifteen-minute wait felt like an hour. Dr. Foster finished the examination and reluctantly admitted that she was baffled by her young patient's symptoms. She suggested the problem might be some kind of flu.

Three days later, each one more painful for Rachel than the day before, her mom called the doctor again with an update.

"Let's take some tests," suggested Dr. Foster.

The tourniquet tight, Rachel watched the needle approach like a stalking lion. She sucked in a breath and closed her eyes, wincing at the bite to her arm.

Two hours later, with multiple vials of blood surrendered, at last Rachel lounged at home in the living room with a book. Now her ankles and wrists ached.

On Sunday evening, Dr. Foster called the house. "The test results didn't show anything. I'd like to consult with another doctor. How is Rachel tonight?"

"She's not doing well," Rachel's mom said. "The pain is worse and seems to be moving to new places."

Rachel captured her protesting five-year-old brother, Zac, in a bear hug. She'd always taken great joy in tickling him. She didn't fight with him like some of her friends did with their little brothers. She actually enjoyed playing with Zac and took every opportunity to tease him and mess with his mop of red hair.

Rachel tried to shove him onto the couch, but hot sparks of pain shot through her wrists. She stumbled onto the cushions, but when Zac pounced on her, crushing stabs in her hips made her cry out in pain.

The dam broke. Rachel was tired of hurting. She burst into tears. She'd dealt with severe allergies and asthma for the last year, sentencing her to two inhalers and banishment from the garden. Ear infections drove her to the doctor often, too, but this pain was more than she could bear. She longed to run and spin on the tire swing again like a normal fourth grader.

Late Monday night, the phone rang and Rachel's mom answered it. Her lips formed a straight line. She nodded, turned her back to Rachel, and said, "Thank you. We'll be there."

"That was Dr. Foster," she said to Rachel in a weary voice. "She wants to run a special test, so we have to go in to town first thing tomorrow."

Rachel felt her mother's anxiety. She had even taken Rachel forward to be anointed with oil and prayed for at church the previous Sunday.

"Be patient," she told Rachel. "God will heal you in His timing."

Rachel trusted God, but she wished He'd hurry up and make her well.

A week later, Rachel was once again sitting in the orange vinyl chair in the clinic waiting room. She fidgeted. The doctor was finally going to tell her what was wrong. Ten minutes later, Dr. Foster met with them in the exam room; a solemn expression guarded her smile.

"At last we have a diagnosis. Rachel has juvenile rheumatoid arthritis. I'm setting up an appointment for her with a specialist." She handed Rachel's mom a thick yellow folder. "I'd like for you to read through this material; then I'll give you a call, say, in two days, to answer any questions you have. I'm so sorry."

Dr. Foster's eyes shone with unshed tears as she gently hugged Rachel, then her mom.

Rachel chewed her lip. She was glad they had an answer at last, but she didn't really know what it meant.

What's wrong with Mom? Why is everyone so serious?

She knew the routine. Next, they would go to the store and pick up a prescription in a brown bottle. Then she'd take a pill for two weeks and feel fine again. She pretended to study the ear chart on the wall while her mom and Dr. Foster talked in low voices; then her mom led her to the car in silence.

When they got home, Rachel noticed that her mom simply tossed the yellow folder on the table. Rachel also saw that she frowned each time she looked at it. Then, when she finally opened the folder, she started crying.

"No cure?" Rachel heard her mom gasp. "Please, God! Not my baby!"

A few days later, Rachel stared at the ceiling, snapping a ponytail holder between her fingers. All of her days were spent on the couch now. Already today, she'd read four books and watched two movies.

She tried to sleep or sit really still so the needles in her joints wouldn't bother her so much. Her mom said they would home-school this year. The unopened box on the table held her new schoolbooks. She didn't know what to expect, but excitement niggled at her like it was Christmas or her birthday.

Every day began the same. Mom scooped Rachel out of the bed, carried her to the bathroom, and then deposited her onto the couch. She tried not to jar or squeeze her, but Rachel winced and held her elbows as she settled into a pile of pillows.

Next came the pills. Rachel hated swallowing all the pills; they made her gag. She missed eating breakfast at the table with Zac and her mom. Every day, without fail, she spilled her cereal on her shirt because sitting up hurt too much. Until her medicine took effect, she just hugged her arms to her chest and tried not to move.

As Rachel waited for her mom to bring her schoolbooks, she watched the floating flames through the glass door of the woodstove. The snap of the freshly stoked fire was like a familiar friend. A friend with a warm embrace whispering, "It's going to be okay."

Weeks melted into months, and Rachel busied herself with movies, reading, and school. Colored leaves rode the breezes, leaving the trees barren. Television holiday specials eased the boredom, but with the decreased mobility came the increased desire to sleep away the pain.

When lunch was over and schoolwork put away for the day, Zac napped. It was time for an afternoon break. Rachel enjoyed this time with her mom each day. They'd watch news and stories on the Christian channel. Sometimes her mom would just sit and hold her, and other times she'd fold clothes.

Rachel's mom stood and stretched, then headed off to put away the clean clothes. Eyelids heavy, Rachel heard a man on the television saying something about arthritis. That got her attention. "Someone watching this right now has arthritis. You are in pain and God is healing you this very minute. Claim this healing for yourself and thank Him for it."

A strange quiver leapt inside her. Rachel believed that God healed sick people. She knew the stories of Jesus healing the blind and crippled. Her pastor and friends at church had prayed for God to heal her. Her mom had told her Jesus would heal her in His timing. Joy filled her heart.

Now is that time! Thank you, Jesus! Thank you for healing me!

Rachel's mom returned to the big chair with another basket of warm clothes fresh from the dryer. Rachel hugged a pillow to her chest and laughed. At first her mom couldn't understand what she was trying to tell her.

"God is healing me!"

Her mom's jaw dropped. She sat on the couch beside Rachel and then held her daughter tighter than she had in months.

"Don't cry, Mama. I'm going to be all better!"

Rachel's mom buried her face in her daughter's rumpled brown hair.

Each night as Rachel closed her eyes to sleep, she fully expected to be pain-free the next morning. But the aches were still there. She knew God was healing her, though, and noticed each day was less painful than the day before.

By the third day, her mom didn't have to carry her. Her hips still hurt, but she could walk. By the fourth day her wrists and ankles stopped aching and she went outside. She grinned as a waft of manure and the crisp smell of hay flooded her senses.

Humming, she gathered eggs and reached into the stall to scratch her pony, Bright Eyes.

Each morning she thought, *Is today the day God will finish healing me?*

Rachel's first painless day came seven days after she prayed with the man on TV. Seven days—the amount of time it took for the arthritis to totally take hold of her body after the first symptoms, four very long months ago.

Rachel wasn't sick one time that entire winter—no colds, ear infections, or flu. She didn't need either of her inhalers that next spring. Her asthma and allergies were gone.

"When God heals a body, He does a perfect job," Rachel's mom said.

Rachel could work in the garden now with her mom because her eyes didn't swell shut.

Rachel stretched to buckle the halter on Bright Eyes. As the sun emerged from its hiding place behind a gray cloud, she shielded her blue eyes with her hand to look into the sky. The sun's rays warmed her cheeks.

"Thank you, God. Thank you for healing me," Rachel whispered. One foot in the stirrup, with a "whoop" she propelled herself into the saddle and kicked the black pony into a trot.

A Belated Good-bye

Linda O'Connell

I was the first grandchild in the family, and Pappy was my best friend. When I was a baby, he would ride the streetcar to my parents' home to pick me up on Friday nights after he got off work. Then he would take me back home on Sunday afternoons.

Pappy and Grandma were so attached to me that Grandma insisted Pappy build a place at the rear of their property for my family to live in. When I was three, we moved in. I was thrilled to be so close to my grandparents.

As a preschooler, I would sit on the front porch with Pappy, waiting for the milk delivery. I'd watch and listen in amazement as he drummed his fingers on the wooden rail.

"The horses are coming. You hear them?"

I was fascinated with his ability to replicate the sound of the milkman clomping by with his horse-drawn wagon filled with glass bottles. Often, Pappy would take me by the hand

and we'd walk slowly to the corner market. He was as proud of me as I was of him.

On my fifth birthday, I walked down the ribbon of concrete walkway that led to my grandparents' house. I entered their house quietly, surprising them.

Grandma reminded Pappy that it was my special day. He reached into his pocket and pulled out a handful of pennies. He counted five into my upturned palm.

"What's the matter with you?" Grandma reprimanded. "This is your granddaughter. What do you mean by giving her only five pennies?"

My Italian grandfather looked shocked and explained, "One penny for each year."

"Nonsense!" my German grandma bellowed. "You give her more than five cents!"

Pappy dumped all of his pennies into my hand. My chubby fist overflowed like the happiness in my heart.

I ran back to our house to show my mom what Pappy had given me. I laid my coins on the nightstand, and Mom said it was bedtime soon.

My younger brother and I slept in our own beds in our parents' bedroom. That night, we were sleeping soundly when the room was illuminated with a blinding flash of light that woke all of us.

"What time is it?" Mom asked.

"Three o'clock," Dad said, looking at the loudly ticking alarm clock. Suddenly a picture fell off the wall behind my parents' bed, and the glass in the frame broke.

Dad said in a hushed tone, "Someone close to us has died."

"Aww, you're crazy and superstitious," my mom said. "It was probably lightning."

"The weather is calm outside," my dad replied as he moved the bed and helped her sweep up the shards of glass. "You mark my words. God sends us warnings, sometimes. The good Lord is capable of miracles." His voice sounded mysterious.

I agreed with Dad. I had been going to Sunday school every week, and I had learned about the fish and loaves and the parting of the Red Sea. Maybe a miracle had happened.

We all settled back down and went to sleep.

Just as dawn was breaking, we were awakened by a knock on the door. Mom's sister told us the bad news: Pappy had died during the night.

I reached for my pile of pennies.

My heart was broken, but I was five and not fully aware of what was going on. The day of the funeral, my brother and I played with our cousins in the funeral parlor.

To be honest, despite my aunts and grandma weeping, I felt like we were at a party. I chased my brother and bumped into an antique brass pole lamp with a gorgeous glass globe. It crashed to the floor, and that ruby shade broke into a million pieces.

My embarrassed and angry mother scrunched up her face and chased us down. With my brother in one hand and me in the other, she parked us in the pew with our father. I sat as quietly as I could, my feet dangling, my body wanting to go up front and look into the casket. I wanted to see Pappy "asleep with Jesus."

When the ushers released visitors in each pew for an organized viewing, I waited anxiously for my turn.

"No! You sit right there and be still!" Dad said.

My parents were in cahoots, and all I could do was stand on tippy-toes and clutch the pew in front of me, hoping to stretch high enough to see inside the casket. I was unable to, and I desperately needed to see my pappy.

I began to sniffle and cry, embarrassing my parents again. Mom, who sat up front with Grandma and five siblings, glared a warning look at me. I sat back down.

When my dad rose to his feet, he ordered my brother and me to remain seated.

I whined and wailed, "I want to go with you. I want to see Pappy, too. It's not fair!"

"No! Sit down. I'll be right back," he commanded.

I wanted my mom, but she was too far away.

"Daddy, please hold me up! I want to see Pappy."

He lifted me briefly, and then he sat me down with a warning not to move a muscle. I had only been able to get a glimpse, which only made me want to see more.

I *had* to go see Pappy.

Just as my heart was thumping and my mind was racing with my bright idea of running down the aisle, Dad returned and scooted me way down the pew next to my brother.

I tried to communicate with Pappy. Somehow. In my child's mind, without speaking aloud, I told him that I loved him. I begged him to let me see him. I told him my parents wouldn't let me come up front.

Silent tears flowed and sobs racked my little body. I was not as sad as I was angry at my inability to have any control.

Reverend Prell, our church pastor, a very kind man, nodded in my direction before commencing the sermon. It was a warning that children should be seen and not heard.

I listened to the sermon, the nice words about my grandfather, the mention of family names. But my eyes were on that casket with the lid still open.

"Pappy, I love you!"

My lips were sealed, but I was shouting within.

The sermon ended, an organ chimed, the scent of funeral flowers and ladies' cologne filled the chapel. Women wearing veiled hats began to shift in their seats and gather their belongings.

I kept my eyes trained on that open casket until the last person meandered by. At that moment, I gasped. A miracle was happening before my very eyes!

Stunned and speechless, I watched Pappy sit up in his silk-lined coffin. He turned his head to the right, and he looked directly at me in the pew.

"Good-bye, my little Linda. I love you, too," he said.

I could see him without even standing on tiptoe. I remained seated, my eyes focused on him. He smiled a smile that had the brilliance of a million birthday candles. Then he laid back down, and the funeral director closed the lid.

My heart overflowed with satisfaction and confusion. The rest of the day was a blur. I kept my secret to myself, and my mind's eye kept revisiting the images of what I had experienced. My daddy was right; the good Lord had just performed a miracle, and I was a witness.

Years later when I told my parents how Pappy had told me good-bye, they laughed and said, "Impossible!" They told me it was my imagination running wild. They acknowledged that I had been a bright and active child with a good vocabulary.

I told Grandma, but she chuckled, too, and said, "Wishful thinking."

For years I could not come up with a logical explanation, and I was unable to convince others of what I had witnessed. School friends laughed at me. So I kept the images in my heart and always at the back of my mind.

When I became an adult and shared my miraculous experience with friends, they told me I must have had a vivid dream.

I smiled and nodded, knowing full well that I knew the difference between vivid dreams and what I had experienced. I'd had those scary chase dreams that were so real I woke up breathless and unable to scream. What happened to me was real; it was not a dream.

I don't share this story with others anymore unless I know they are believers in the gifts God dispenses to even the youngest of His believers. I don't question *how* it happened. I just know that on a June day in the mid-1950s, it happened for me.

Jesus Played With Me!

Verda J. Glick

"Armed robbers hid behind our house last evening," our son Paul said when I answered the telephone early one morning. His voice sounded strained. "They jumped out at us when we got home after dark. They ordered me to unlock the door, forced their way into the house with us, and made us sit down under guard while they ransacked the house."

"Oh no, Paul! No! I'm so sorry! Did they hurt you?"

"No, Mama, but they stole our money, computer, camera, and other things. I couldn't call you sooner because they stole our phones. I waited until daylight to go to a neighbor to borrow a phone to call you. Geneva and I hardly slept last night."

My eyes filled with tears. All too familiar with the trauma of armed robberies, my husband and I had hoped our children would be spared. Now Paul and his family had been targeted, too. It hurt much worse than when it happened to us.

Paul and his wife, Geneva, live on a small farm in El Salvador with their son and daughter, five-year-old Jacinto and two-year-old Kenia. Paul serves as director of the church choir. The family had returned to their home after choir practice the previous evening. That's when the robbers assaulted them.

I brushed away the tears that kept coming.

"Do you think they're the same robbers who've been coming here to rob us?" I asked, trying to control the tremor in my voice.

"Yes, it really does seem like the same bunch. The appearance of these men matches your description of the ones who have robbed you. The way they forced their way into the house and made us sit under guard while they ransacked the house sounds just like what you've experienced lately."

Concern for our young grandchildren seized me. "Are the children all right?"

"Yes, they're okay. Kenia doesn't seem too upset. I don't think she understood what was happening."

"What about Jacinto?"

"He fell asleep on the way home, and he slept through the whole thing. We had to leave him sleeping outside in the pickup when the robbers ordered me to unlock the house."

I gasped. "Oh! How awful! Weren't you afraid to do that?"

"Yes, it was terribly hard to leave Jacinto out there all that time. But the men forced Geneva, Kenia, and me to go inside with them and leave Jacinto in the truck. Fortunately, he didn't wake up. It took the men about thirty minutes to search our house and gather all the things they wanted to take. Finally, when the robbers left, I went out, picked up Jacinto, and put him to bed. He kept on sleeping. I'm really glad he didn't wake up and see the men and their guns."

"Yes, that's good," I agreed. "He would have been very frightened. He's such a sensitive child."

"Let's try never to talk about the incident in Jacinto's hearing. Geneva and I hope he won't find out and worry about it."

But Jacinto did find out. And he did worry.

"Daddy, the bad men won't come tonight, will they?" he would ask each night when darkness fell.

Even on warm nights Jacinto covered himself completely with a sheet, pulling it up over his head in order to feel safer.

"God, don't let the bad men come tonight," he prayed night after night. Afraid of the dark, he always wanted a night-light by his bed.

In the daytime, his fear of robbers dominated his play. "Here come the bad men with their guns! They're going to shoot. Call the police! Oh! Here come the police. The bad men are running away!"

Weeks passed. Jacinto kept playing out his imaginary cops-and-robbers games. He kept asking if the bad men would come. And he kept praying that God would keep the robbers away.

One morning, two months after the robbery, Jacinto ran out of his bedroom.

"Mommy!" he called. "I heard a noise, so I stood on my bed and looked out the window. I saw angels! The bad men were scared and ran away."

Geneva paused as she set the table for breakfast. "That was a nice dream you had, Jacinto," she said.

"No, Mommy," Jacinto insisted. "It wasn't a dream. I was awake. The bad men made a noise that woke me up. It was *not* a dream. I saw lots and lots of angels in the yard."

"What did they look like?"

"They wore bright shiny clothes. And they had big knives, much bigger than the bad men's knives. The bad men were afraid of the angels, and they ran away. Fast!" Jacinto's eyes shone with excitement. "Mommy, one of the angels stood on the power line. The rest stood in the yard with their big knives." He pointed toward heaven. "Then they all went up."

She shook her head. "It sounds like a dream."

"No, Mommy. It wasn't a dream. It was real. Then Jesus came right through the door." Jacinto pointed to the closed front door. "He didn't open it. He just came through it. He talked with me, and He played with me. He was so nice. I really liked playing with Him. He told me He'll come back again."

Jacinto still talks about bad men, and he still plays games of cops chasing robbers. But he doesn't cover his head at night anymore. And darkness has stopped being scary.

One night recently when returning from choir practice, Geneva exclaimed, "Oh, dear! I forgot to turn on the front porch light before we left home. We'll have to go inside in the dark!"

Jacinto said, "Ah, Mommy. Why are you always so afraid of the dark?"

After all, he knows God's angels stand on guard, they have big knives, and the bad men are afraid of them. And Jesus is his friend and is always very near.

The Sanctuary Light

James Stuart Bell

I am the firstborn son of a couple of intelligent and self-made parents who were climbing the social and economic ladder when I was young. They just assumed I was precocious and, by twisting a few arms, broke the rules to get me into two different "spheres of influence" a year early.

The athletic and spiritual orbits thus witnessed the debut of James Stuart Bell Jr. at the tender age of seven instead of eight.

You might assume parents like this would fit the high-pressure and ambitious types that would cause their child to eventually break down because he was never good enough. But that was not the case. They were, in fact, easygoing and loving parents who wanted to take advantage of opportunities in life from the get-go. And they gave me the choice—I didn't have to join either activity a year early. But I looked forward to the challenge and accepted both offers.

The early Little League start helped me to do fairly well in baseball and gave me a lifetime love of the sport (the St. Louis Cardinals, in particular). I still have the baseball from when I pitched a victory that allowed more runs than hits. My dad became manager a couple of years later but still had the gentle touch, as well as fairness, and tried not to show me any favoritism.

In terms of the spiritual domain, I entered the lowest rank (unordained) of Catholic clergy at the age of *seven*. It was just before Vatican II, and altar boys had to be a hardy lot. We had an important job, especially with cruets of water and wine and, sometimes, burning briquettes of incense in a holder to be swung around the altar in special services.

I was so short that I would trip over the smallest cassock, and when we had to kneel I couldn't get back up. But since we assisted at the 6:30 a.m. Mass, not that many people were there, or they weren't awake enough to notice.

My main challenge as a whippersnapper altar boy was not to fall asleep and not to pass out. Why the latter? Because the pre-Vatican rules said no eating or drinking (except water) before receiving Communion. One morning, famished on an empty stomach and half-asleep, I was kneeling with my eyes closed and head down into my lily-white surplice. I opened my eyes and everything was still black. And then I looked like the Leaning Tower of Pisa and toppled over.

Perhaps the biggest challenge was learning the prayers in Latin. I was really too young for that kind of foreign memorization. When we had to say our confession of sin, as I knelt I would bow low and say, "*Confiteor Deo omnipotenti. . . .*" (I confess to almighty God.) Then I would bow even lower and mumble a few of the Latin words of the confession and get away with it.

That's where I was spiritually at the time, following everything by rote in my Catholic school world and trying to do what I was told. (A couple of years later I got smacked at my desk by Sister Floriana, and I still don't know what I did wrong or didn't do right.)

Up to that time I knew nothing of anything immoral. I lived in a safe, prosperous middle-class neighborhood in a loving family, where we watched sitcoms featuring families like ours who had very small conflicts and quick happy endings. Poverty and race issues were out in the stratosphere somewhere, and it wasn't until the following year that the Civil Rights Movement really took hold and the Vietnam War right after that.

So when November 22, 1963, announced itself, my world was rocked by two events in two days.

The first event was illness. The previous day I had gone into the hospital for a bladder operation. I was quite anxious because at ten years of age I had never been in a hospital for an operation. My mother had a difficult time convincing me that I would ever wake up again if I went to sleep apart from my own will.

The next morning, they gave me some ice cream and I went home. Shortly after we arrived, I yelled to my mother when leaving the bathroom that I was still in some pain from the operation. And then I heard what I thought were sobs coming from behind her bedroom door.

"Don't worry, Mom. It doesn't hurt that bad!" I shouted.

But when she called me into her room, I could see she was shattered. She told me she'd heard from my dad on the phone that President Kennedy had been shot and had died. So the second earth-shattering event was the murder of our thirty-fifth president.

I simply couldn't comprehend the enormity of this horrific deed. We were Irish-American and were very proud of our president and his family. Why would anyone want to end his life?

I tried to make sense of evil in the world as my family and I later watched the assassination of Lee Harvey Oswald on live television.

A couple of months later, evil personally hit home. We had heard about a few recent kidnappings in the Chicago area.

Then our neighbor across the street called my mother and told her to keep me under close watch—her little boy had been solicited in her front yard by a man in a car who promised the little tyke some candy if he would go for a ride. The mom opened her front door and he "took off like a bird." (To this day, over fifty years later, I still remember the phrase she used to describe the driver leaving the scene.)

My mother had warned me since I was five to *never* speak to a stranger alone. Now the ominous message had a major impact upon me. She spelled out the possible dire consequences of my little friend taking that ride, and I could see she was fearful for me.

I suddenly became paranoid of strangers and even cars. I would check under the bed at night and listen for outside noises. When I got off the bus after school, I would walk through the backyards of neighbors to avoid any confrontation with strangers. When my sister and I were left in the car, we made sure to lock the doors.

This dark cloud remained upon me as we moved into the Lenten season of 1964. I was asking God why all these bad things were happening, and as a result, I was learning to pray. I was now seeking freedom from fear and the knowledge that God cared and was in control.

As a now "veteran" altar boy, I was asked to be a server for the forty-hour devotions as part of the Lenten season in our church. Someone would remain in prayer in front of the altar during the entire forty-hour period.

I got a one-hour afternoon shift, and because our church was connected to the school, I was thrilled to get an hour out of class to keep the devotions going unabated.

There I knelt down directly in front of the little side altar, hands folded up toward the sky, with the perfect Prince Charles haircut my mother insisted upon, uniform with school crest under cassock and surplice, black prayer book on the little armrest.

I was "holding the fort" in solemn vigil, alone in the church. Just me and God. Was He really present in a special way with just *me*?

In the midst of these changes in life, I knew God was real, but He was way up there somewhere, possibly waiting for me to make another mistake. My parents and spiritual leaders had also told me He was pure and unlimited love. I gritted my teeth, squinted my eyes, and begged God to make himself real to me, to take away the unsettledness of months past.

Then suddenly, with my eyes closed, I felt a tingling sensation and something boring gently into the middle of my forehead. (Something I still feel from God occasionally to this day.) I felt a great sense of peace and love washing gently over me.

"Is that you, Jesus?"

I opened my eyes, and the large red sanctuary lamp seemed to be vividly ablaze, searing me with its reality. It was like a welcoming beacon in a storm, drawing me to it with its warmth and power.

He's not an uninterested God way out in the cosmos; He's in me and right here in front of me, wanting to love and care for me, I thought.

That experience was the bedrock of my initial personal faith. After Communion, for a number of Sundays that year, I felt the same sensations as I prayed in my pew. I remained an altar boy and finally became head altar boy at seventeen years old.

Though I lost my faith for a short time after that in college, I returned to have an even more powerful encounter at twenty, and remain with Him once and for all.

Many years later, when my mother passed away, her funeral card listed her favorite Scripture passage—Psalm 27:1: "The Lord is my light and my salvation—whom shall I fear?" (NIV).

When I realized in that church sanctuary that Jesus is the light of my life, my fear was dispelled. His light always overcomes the darkness.

A Special Visitation

Sandra L. Hickman

"It's a miracle!" the nurse declared to the weary new parents. They were so inexperienced. In the eye of the storm, during the long delivery process, they had been emotionally ravaged and shell-shocked.

In disbelief, the doctor announced, "If this amazing improvement continues, he can go home in four days!"

The neurologist stated, "I don't know why or how, but your baby has survived! It's a miracle he's even alive . . . and it can only be from above!" He gestured his hand toward heaven.

Spastic cerebral palsy was the heartbreaking legacy of Jordan's difficult and prolonged birth. His brain having suffered severe trauma and damage, he was considered unlikely to survive. But God has done awesome and amazing supernatural things from his birth until now.

The prayer chains for Jordan went around Australia. Family and friends in other states and territories were all praying for the baby in Western Australia. Even people who didn't know him prayed for Jordan.

And God heard!

The doctors said he wouldn't live; then they said he wouldn't talk or have any intellect. More than two decades later, all of Jordan's limbs and muscles are stiffened and tight. His hands and feet are twisted and rigid due to spasticity. He walks with a peculiar gait and has slightly slurred speech. However, his intelligence is normal.

Though they said he wouldn't live, Jordan has a zeal for life like none other. Jordan smiles and the world stops! His sense of humor is amazing. His heart is as beautiful as his personality.

Those of us around Jordan have witnessed numerous miracles in his life from the time he was born. Yet, while Jordan was still young, God proved something amazing to him. God had His own special awesome miracle just for him as a very young child.

The miracle happened when a kind friend gifted Jordan's family with a weeklong holiday at a resort in their hometown of Mandurah, Western Australia.

Daddy had gone to work that morning. Everyone else was sleeping—Mummy and the three children, Jordan, age nine, Eligh, age six, and Isabella, age three. It was quiet at the holiday resort since this was the off-peak winter season.

Jordan was the first to wake after his dad left, so he got up. He sat alone in the living room, quietly watching television, when someone knocked at the chalet door.

Jordan stood, wondering who was there. Puzzled that Mummy and the little ones had not awakened at the noise, he tentatively walked toward the door with his usual frail, faltering gait. Wondering whether or not he should open it, he just took that little leap of childlike faith and turned the knob with his tiny twisted hands.

A white light flooded into the chalet. It was so bright that at first it hurt Jordan's eyes. Then Jordan saw *Him*! Jesus stood in the doorway! The white light was surrounding and shining so brightly from Him that Jordan was awestruck. This was *Jesus*. And He was there for an audience with Jordan!

Jordan later told his mum of his incredible experience.

"Why did Jesus come to *me*?" he asked her.

"Jordan, I think that Jesus knocking on the door of the chalet means that He was knocking on the door of your heart. He wants to come in!" she replied.

Later that day, while preparing to play tennis, the children were excitedly talking to Mummy about how Jesus had knocked on the door. They said, "Mum, we want to invite Jesus into our hearts."

They planned that after tennis they would sit together and do it. But their mummy heard the Holy Spirit say, "Now—not later!"

So that's what they did.

The children were eager with questions: "How do we do it? Can we have worship first, Mum?"

They decided to each choose one song. During worship the children all felt God's awesome presence.

"Mum, what is this?" cried Eligh.

Mummy explained about the Holy Spirit. They all sang with hands held upward and tears on their cheeks. Mummy led them in prayer as Jordan, Eligh, and Isabella gave their hearts to Jesus. What a glorious time they shared!

The chalet visitation was not the only one for Jordan. Just weeks later, he had a dream in which he was again with Jesus.

Jordan sat Mummy down and said, "I was standing, and a white light came down and went into me, and then I was running! I was not a cerebral palsy boy anymore, Mum! I looked and Jesus was running with me! Then Jesus said to me, 'I am going to use you to do things that others can't.'"

Jordan continued, "Jesus took me to a big street. Everywhere I looked I saw people who were sick, in wheelchairs, on beds, all kinds of sickness! Jesus told me which people to touch. He would say, 'This one.' And when I touched the people, they were healed."

"What did you say to Jesus?" Jordan's mum asked.

"Mum, I didn't speak to Jesus!" Jordan replied with his eyes wide open. "I am just His servant. He spoke to me. Jesus told me what to do, and I did it."

Jordan spoke with new maturity as though his dream were a normal occurrence. He was so confident that he had been with Jesus once again—just like the visitation at the chalet door!

There is much more to Jordan's story. I wish you could have known him when he was a brave little boy, and witnessed the struggles and victories. He has received several healings in his body that medical professionals cannot explain. A life full of miracles big and small have woven the fabric of who he is today—this person God so fearfully and wonderfully made.

Jordan sees life as something to be enjoyed, not endured, and he gives much more than he takes from it. To look at Jordan is to see God's amazing grace in motion. It's as if the Lord is saying, "Watch this space; keep looking, because you will witness something amazing taking place."

Jesus talks to children, and through Jordan we learned to never doubt when they speak about their encounters with the Lord Jesus Christ. Jordan just told it how it was. It happened, he knew it, he believed it—nothing complicated, just the facts spoken with the truth and innocence of a child.

A Welcome Friend

Laura L. Bradford

"Grandma!" I shouted, slamming the kitchen door behind me.
"A friend came to play with me."

Turning away from her pile of laundry, my grandmother
gave me a questioning look. She realized that the only possible
playmate living near our isolated property was a girl in her late
teens. But Judy had never shown an interest in playing with
four-year-old kids like me.

"Who would have come all the way out here to play with
you?" she asked.

"I don't know his name," I answered, "but he was really fun,
like Daddy used to be."

"Your friend is . . . a guy?" Grandma asked, looking pale.
"Was he a grown-up?"

"Yup. And he came just to see me," I bragged. "He stepped
out from behind the clothesline pole. Then he told me all

about Daddy while we played hide-and-seek in the sheets on the clotheslines."

"No-o-o!" Grandma cried. "I'm not going to let anyone hurt my baby!"

Grabbing her butcher knife, my arthritic grandmother hobbled toward the door.

"But, Grandma," I begged, tugging on her arm, "you don't have to go out there 'cause he's gone now. He stepped back behind the clothesline pole and disappeared."

"No he didn't," she growled, charging though the doorway. "It's not possible for anyone to do that. He's probably still lurking out there somewhere, so I'm going to find that beast and cut him to bits!"

"No, Grandma, stop!" I said. "He was re-e-eally nice."

But Grandma kept hobbling toward the clotheslines, going faster than I'd ever seen her move. Holding the butcher knife high in the air, she gasped for breath with every step. A couple of times, she almost fell when she tripped on sticks, rocks, or lumps in the grass.

I begged Grandma to stop, but she kept going. Why wouldn't she believe that my friend was a nice guy and that he'd already gone away? I found it frustrating to make grown-ups understand me.

But then, I had trouble understanding grown-ups, too. I didn't know why my father had quit coming home. I missed him so much that I'd sit by the kitchen window during suppertime, watching for his car to come up the driveway. My mother and grandmother would try to pull me away from the window, saying, "You've got to stop starving yourself, Laura. Your daddy is dead. He's not coming home—not ever again."

My older sister would say the same words, but I didn't know what they meant.

Over and over I tried to explain, "Daddy always comes home to me. Always. So I'm staying by the window. When he gets home, I'll eat."

After my knife-wielding grandmother had searched all around our clotheslines, I followed her all over the yard while she looked everywhere for my friend. When she found nothing, she grabbed my hand and dragged me toward the house.

"You're not playing outside for the rest of the day," she announced. "Maybe not for the rest of the week. I won't allow some dirty old man to hurt my baby."

"But, Grandma," I explained, "he wasn't dirty at all. His clothes were really white, whiter than your sheets. And he wasn't very old either. He was young and skinny, like Uncle Bud. And his face was really nice. It was brighter than his clothes."

Grandma stopped in her tracks. Turning to look me in the eye, she asked, "You say his clothes were white? They were totally white?"

"Yup," I answered, nodding, "and his hair too."

I was afraid to say any more since Grandma had such a worried look on her face.

After that, my friend returned a few more times. He came one night when I was longing to have my dad lift me up so I could see my mother's china pieces on the fireplace mantel. While I stood in the living room next to my father's huge recliner, the friend came and did exactly what my father would have done. He picked me up and carried me to the mantel.

As I dangled high in the air, I remember being aware that I had to "mind my manners," as Dad always said. I wasn't supposed to touch any of the china pieces. My friend carried me from one side of the mantel to the other until I was satisfied that I'd seen everything. Then he placed me back on the floor.

Excited to tell everyone about my adventure, I dashed into the kitchen and said, "My friend came to lift me up just like Daddy used to do."

Sis glared at me and growled, "You're crazy."

Mom ran out of the kitchen crying. But my grandmother seemed to understand. She just grinned. Then she gave me a wink.

Years later, my visiting friend did what my father *never* could have done. While I played alone outside, longing for my father, the friend lifted me up again.

That time I was high enough to look down on our house. I remember studying the artistic layout of the shingles and seeing leaves and twigs caught in the crevices near the dormers.

Once he'd placed me back on the ground, I was overjoyed to know that I wasn't alone. Even though my father hadn't come home, someone still cared about me.

I wouldn't remember any of my encounters with that friendly visitor if it weren't for my grandmother. A woman of faith, with a gift of discernment, she eventually realized that my friend was no mortal man. She also reminded me of his visits. Repeatedly she told me of the miraculous transformation that took place shortly after my first encounter with my visitor at the clotheslines. Evidently, something that he communicated to me made me quit waiting by the window for my father, who had perished in a car accident. Instead, I started joining the family for meals once again.

Over time I came to understand that my visitor is the best friend anyone could have and that His heart's desire is to give everyone access to His Father—a father who will never die. My friend's name is Jesus.

"To Keep Thee in All Thy Ways"

Catherine Ulrich Brakefield

The snow slapped my windowpane with icy fingers in rhythm with the howling wind.

The slaps reminded me of my first-grade teacher, who was fond of slapping her hands when she wasn't happy. Her scowling face sneaked into my memory, her high-pitched voice echoing in my ears. "Don't come to school tomorrow without your crayons."

I burrowed deeper into my blankets and glanced at the picture of a massive white angel directing a little girl and boy across a rickety bridge. One wrong step and they would tumble over that swaying bridge into the rapids beneath it. That angel really had his work cut out for him.

My younger sisters and I had received the painting as a Christmas present weeks earlier. And that morning Mother had read

Matthew 18:10 from our new children's Bible, telling us Jesus loves all His children: "Their angels in heaven always see the face of my Father in heaven."

Mom said we had a guardian angel of our very own. All we needed to do was call on Jesus and He'd come to our rescue.

"Cathy, get dressed!" Mom yelled from downstairs. "Your father's driving you to school today on his way to work."

I donned the clothes Mom had set out for me to wear and hurried downstairs. Bacon sizzled in the cast-iron skillet, and the tantalizing aroma filled the room. Baby Diana in her wooden high chair banged her spoon on her tray. My sister, Peg, was sampling the jam and biscuits.

Dad scanned the headlines of the *Detroit News*, flipping the pages to the business section while sopping up his egg yolks with one of Mom's flaky biscuits.

I bit into Mom's biscuit layered with homemade grape jam, then started on my egg. The wind rattled the kitchen window-panes. It reminded me of Miss Ward's long fingers and pointed nails that could slap together at a moment's notice and belittle a rowdy student with a well-directed smack.

I looked at my half-eaten breakfast and said, "Are you sure there's school, Mom? It sounds awful bad outside. Who's going to pick me up?"

"I will, hon." Mom swept a soft kiss on my brow. "Peg's kindergarten class has been cancelled, but elementary school hasn't."

Baby Diana's banging became louder. "Mom, I could stay home and help you."

Mom replaced Diana's spoon with toast. "No, I don't think so. Here is your book satchel and lunch. I put your box of crayons in your lunch box." She leaned over and kissed me again.

"Nibs (she addressed my dad), I can't see the need of reprimanding a little girl for forgetting something as trivial as crayons."

"Perseverance, Margaret." Dad glanced at me and then to my mom. "After all, I went to parochial schools all the way through high school. Believe me, I learned never to forget anything."

Dad took a final sip of his coffee. Then his chair grated across the linoleum floor, signaling that my time to bask in the homey atmosphere was over.

"Nibs, she hasn't finished eating," Mom said to my dad. Her warm palm felt my head. "Maybe she has a fever. . . . No, you feel OK."

"Cathy, hurry up." Dad had his coat on and was holding the door open for me. Mom helped me get my new galoshes on. I put on my coat, hat, and mittens, and then clutched my book satchel and lunch box to my chest. I could not escape the inevitable. As I climbed into our Ford, my feet weighed a ton.

The sound of the windshield wipers mingled with the howling wind outside the car. Wispy funnels of snow swirled in front of the car's headlights.

I leaned forward. I couldn't see the side of the road. Only the taillights of the car two feet ahead were visible. Dad glanced at his wristwatch. "Your school is just four blocks away, and it's taken fifteen minutes to get this far."

As we turned the corner, the road stretched bumper to bumper with cars and buses cramming the snow-covered school road. The traffic light blinked amber before my eyes, and the two-story brick building of my school appeared in view. I swallowed. What would Miss Ward find to get mad at me about today?

Dad checked his wristwatch again. "I'm late."

The light turned red. The traffic was snarled, and no car had made it through.

"I can cross with the light, Dad. You don't need to drive up to the school. See, the road is clear to the right."

"Are you sure? You just have to cross when the guard tells you. You can do that?"

"Sure." I opened my passenger door and smiled at him. *After all, if I can withstand Miss Ward for six hours a day, I can cross this road.*

"Well, OK."

The school guard nodded as I waited at the curb. I waved as Dad stuck his hand out the window and continued down the road. I crossed with the other children. Then I walked around the school to the side door where Mom always dropped me off.

Suddenly, I slipped. My book satchel flew across the yard. Books went everywhere, as did my lunch box. My sandwich and box of crayons spilled into the snow.

The school bell chimed. Five minutes left. Kids ran around me, stepping on my crayons and sandwich.

A boy laughed as he said, "Oops!"

My crayons lay broken and wet. I knelt over them, and as tears formed in my eyes, I could visualize Miss Ward's angry face staring at me. I blinked and tried to wipe the snow off my crayons.

I was alone. Everyone had gone inside. Stuffing everything into my bag, I got up, walked to the door, and peered inside the school. The hallway was empty. Then I heard Miss Ward's voice.

Her shrieks rose above the howling wind. "Get those wet boots off this instant. You're getting the floor wet!"

I looked down at my snow-covered clothes. *Miss Ward will be furious at me. Plus I'm late, and now my crayons are ruined.* Her voice echoed in my memory: *"Don't come to school without your crayons!"*

I looked around. The traffic light blinked its yellow glow across the snowy landscape. *I got here by myself. I can get home by myself.*

Squaring my shoulders, I headed toward the road and home.

Crossing the road wasn't difficult. Now that school had started, much of the traffic was gone.

I looked around. I walked to the first street and looked up. *Where is Stozenfield?*

The street signs were covered in ice and snow. Everything looked different. Snow whipped across my face and burned my eyes. I tried to wipe the snow from my eyelashes. My wool mittens weren't much help because little ice balls now stuck to them like glue.

Which way is home?

How had Mom said to call my guardian angel? *Oh, I remember, tell Jesus and claim Psalm 91:11—"For he shall give his angels charge over thee, to keep thee in all thy ways"* (KJV).

"Jesus, I'm not sure which road to go down. Could you send my guardian angel, please?" I whispered.

I looked around. Everything was so—white.

"Jesus, I'm not sure I can see my guardian angel in the snow. Can you have him tell me where to go?"

I turned to the left, then to the right.

"There it is . . . that's the road. Thank you, Jesus."

I lowered my head against the pounding wind and walked right into a snowdrift and fell on my face. If I thought everything looked white before, it was even whiter now. . . and a lot colder.

I got up, walked down the road, and turned the corner. One road led to another; I felt someone guiding me, directing my steps.

I didn't know if I was on the sidewalk or how many cars were on the road. The snow was falling faster, layering my clothes, and the wind made the flying flakes feel like sharp needles to my exposed skin. I didn't want to fall again, but I couldn't look up—my face ached from the sharp pricks.

A voice told me to turn. I stumbled but didn't fall; my guardian angel was on duty. I recalled Psalm 91:12, "They shall bear thee up in their hands, lest thou dash thy foot against a stone" (KJV).

I concentrated on watching my red galoshes and putting one foot in front of the other. My hands were so cold I couldn't feel the strap of my book satchel and lunch box. *Did I lose them?*

I looked down. *Thank you, Jesus.* I still had them.

Then the voice told me to look up. There was my house. Tears wet my cheeks as I walked up the steps and opened the kitchen door. "Mom, I'm home."

Mom's eyes grew large as goose eggs. "You look like a miniature snowman! What happened?"

As she helped me discard my wet clothes, I explained about my crayons and why I couldn't go to school.

"I think there is something more than just losing crayons that makes you not want to go to Miss Ward's class. Come on. Let's get you dressed, and I will drive you to school."

"Mom, I can't! My crayons! And Miss Ward will be mad if I come to school late."

Mom helped me into my coat and repacked my satchel. "You won't be alone; I'm going with you."

"Mom, I know. I asked Jesus to send me my angel, and he helped me get home."

Mom laughed. "Well, he did a grand job. Not too many grown-ups could have done what you did today, walking in this blizzard. Your father called and said he couldn't see but two feet ahead driving into work and almost missed the company driveway."

"So—maybe I should stay." I looked hopefully up at her.

Mom laughed. "No, my mind is made up. And since your guardian angel is on duty today, I have nothing better to do than visit with Principal Baker."

Miss Ward was not happy to see me, especially when Principal Baker walked into the classroom and asked to speak with her.

I cringed in my wooden chair and felt like my ears were ringing. But my guardian angel was still on duty just like Mom said. When Miss Ward returned to her classroom, she gave me the biggest smile I had ever seen on her thin lips.

During story time, I shared my morning experience with my classmates and Miss Ward. I explained that they could have a guardian angel. All they had to do was ask Jesus to assign them one.

Miss Ward clapped. Only this time it was for joy.

Miss Ward became much nicer after the snowstorm. Jesus has a way of making everyone feel better—or maybe Miss Ward was afraid Jesus wouldn't assign her a guardian angel if she *wasn't* nice!

Life Is Like a Ball of Yarn

Tracey Dale-Akamine

We entered the hospital room to see my brother, David, who had been admitted for bowel complications—or were they drug-related complications? David had been using drugs for nearly forty years. Sometimes he was off the drugs, sometimes on, but his life never seemed to be headed in an upward direction for very long.

Both of our girls had seen Uncle David in many stages of his addiction—from clean and sober to homeless on the streets. Our oldest daughter, Hannah, always seemed to have his number from the first time she met him. As a little girl of three, she spoke truth into his life: "Uncle David, why do you do drubs? Don't you know they will hurt you? Don't you know when you do drubs Mommy and Nana cry?"

She was relentless in her questioning him that first day she met him. This continued as she grew up and he remained addicted. I remember her once asking me about the "drubs."

"Mommy, why does Uncle David do drubs?"

"I don't know, honey," I said.

"Are they like his God?" she asked.

"Yes, honey, I think to him they are."

"But Mommy, we know there is only one true God," she said.

"Yes, honey, we do." Her understanding was simply amazing at such an early age.

On this particular day when we visited Uncle David, Hannah seemed different—not preoccupied, just introspective, I suppose. Uncle David lay in his hospital bed. My husband, my younger daughter, Nana, and I were at his bedside. Hannah was off to the side, tucked away in the corner.

David chattered as usual, blaming the world for his problems, attacking the hospital staff for their inattentiveness and lack of food options.

Then the conversation shifted. David started to tell us of a dream he'd had the night before. He'd dreamed of a cat playing with a ball of yarn. The cat kept batting it around and around. It rolled farther and farther across the floor until it got pushed behind a door.

"Funny," he said, and he described distinctly seeing the cat's paws from the other side of the door, poking and prodding, trying to bat at the yarn ball unsuccessfully from under and behind the closed door.

"What does it mean?" he asked. When we didn't respond, he kept saying, "What does it mean?" each time louder than before.

This is when I noticed that Hannah seemed uncomfortable. She looked perplexed and fidgety. When my eyes met Hannah's, she motioned for me to meet her in the hall.

"Mommy, I think I know what the dream means," she said. "I think God just spoke to me about the meaning of the dream."

"Really, honey? God spoke to you?" I asked, trusting that He in fact had spoken, because this would not be a first-time encounter with God for her.

"Let's go tell Uncle David," I said.

"No, he may get mad at me."

"Hannah, if God gave you a word to share, it's your responsibility to share it," I replied.

Hannah understood that anytime God spoke to her heart, He may have a specific mission or task for her to fulfill, and this was an opportunity to be used by Him.

Reluctantly, Hannah followed me back into the hospital room. David's chattering was irritating.

"David," I interrupted as he talked right over me. "David, Hannah knows what your dream means."

Finally there was temporary silence.

"What?" he asked.

"Hannah, tell Uncle David what God said the dream means."

Sheepishly Hannah began.

"Uncle David, you are the cat," she said. Her voice began to get a bit louder, but her eyes began to fill with tears. "The ball of yarn is your life. God is trying to tell you that you have been playing around with your life like it is a toy. God is trying to tell you that at any time He can take it from you, and it will be out of your reach. He's trying to tell you to get your life right with Him and get it on the right path before it's too late."

David tried to sit up. He began to cry at the words of his ten-year-old niece. We all were astonished that she could be so articulate and direct.

Within seconds there was not a dry eye in the room. The Lord's presence was so eminent. We all felt the Holy Spirit and were moved to tears.

David agreed with her. "I know, Hannah, you're right," he said. "I have to get my life together with the Lord. Thank you, thank you, Hannah."

We all learned a lesson that day. We all were reminded that God is at work all of the time and that He uses whomever He wants whenever He wants. He used our little girl in an amazing way that afternoon. We were moved by her words and hoped that this would be a new beginning for Uncle David.

Putting Him First

Debra McCann

My daughter, Catherine, has always loved dolphins. You can only imagine how excited I was to be able to tell her that for summer vacation we were going to SeaWorld, and she would be able to see real live dolphins for the first time.

I'll never forget the look on her face when I gave her the news—it was all she could talk about for weeks. Everyone from school and church and all our relatives were so excited for her and smiled when she could not stop talking about the dolphins.

About a week before we were scheduled to leave, I sat down with Catherine to go over the details of the trip and to prepare her for what was coming. She has intellectual disabilities and is uncomfortable with anything unexpected. She likes to know exactly what will happen, or else she worries about it way too much.

When I told Catherine we would leave on Saturday and go to SeaWorld on Sunday I was shocked at her response.

"No, Mother, I do not want to go," she said.

I panicked. I never would have been able to afford a trip like this, but a promotional contest at work included SeaWorld as a participating business where I could use any points I won during the contest. The hotel package included breakfast with Shamu and SeaWorld tickets for one day. But to use the package, one of the days of our trip had to be Sunday, which meant we would need to get on the road early Saturday and skip church on Sunday.

I didn't have a problem missing church, but Catherine did. I started speaking in a way parents sometimes do when they want to talk their kids into doing something.

She was not falling for it.

After several attempts, I finally said, "Catherine, would you rather go see the dolphins and whales and go swimming, or would you rather go to church?"

"I'd rather go to church."

Catherine has dolphins everywhere around her—on bath towels, rugs, knickknacks, pictures, jewelry, you name it. She even has a handmade quilt with dolphins on it from her Great-Aunt Carol. I thought Catherine loved dolphins and whales more than anything.

I was wrong; she loves God even more.

In the following days, I tried to convince her. She stood firm that she would rather be in church. I couldn't help but think of the Scripture that says, "A little child shall lead them" (Isaiah 11:6 KJV).

I eventually gave in to her wishes and cancelled the SeaWorld trip. That summer we ended up going to a small resort town called Lewes, Delaware. It was a lot closer, and we did not have to miss church because we could leave right after the services were over.

When we checked into the hotel, the clerk asked if we had seen all the commotion at the canal. We hadn't noticed anything as we drove near the hotel. He suggested we walk over to the canal, about a block away, and see the dolphins.

I couldn't believe it—dolphins were actually swimming in the canal right by our hotel. We walked over to see them as soon as we were unpacked.

Later that day we went to the grocery store and the cashier asked if we'd seen the dolphins. We told him we had.

"There've been marine biologists coming to town to try to figure out why the dolphins are here and how they got into the canal," he told us. "We've never had dolphins in that canal before."

All I know is that every day we were there, Catherine got to see real live dolphins. She was amazed and so happy. I think God brought the dolphins there because Catherine honored God. As Psalm 37:4 says, "Delight yourself in the Lord, and he will give you the desires of your heart" (ESV).

Of course, God did not stop there. We decided to go to Sea-World the next year, leaving after church and checking into the hotel late. Even though it was early evening, Catherine was so excited about SeaWorld that we went to the park that night.

When we first arrived at SeaWorld, we had to get something to eat because we had been on the road for several hours. The restaurant was amazing—as soon as you walked in, your eyes were drawn to the beautiful displays of fruits and desserts. I don't even remember what we ordered because when we got to the register, there was a problem.

After we'd waited about five minutes, the manager said, "You're in luck; your meals are free because the system is down."

We didn't get to see a lot of the park before it closed for the evening, but we made sure we saw the dolphins!

The next day we went to SeaWorld again and expected to purchase tickets since we had used our tickets the night before. I gave our tickets to the woman at the counter so we could pay the discounted price for this return trip, and she waved us to go ahead. I told her we'd used the tickets the night before, so we needed to buy today's tickets.

She looked at them and said, "You came in late last night, so just go ahead."

We did not have to pay for tickets that day and spent the entire day and evening there. Catherine had a wonderful time and still remembers it.

I still remember how God continued to pour out His blessings. And I believe He did so because of her decision to put Him first—a lesson I will never forget.

Encounter at the Graveyard

Valerie Avery

Pop! Another can of beer opened. I hated that sound! My parents' voices got louder and louder the more they drank.

And the more they drank, the more frightened I became. I hid in my bedroom to stay safe.

Maybe I can spend the night at my grandmother's house. It's safe there. Should I risk asking Dad to take me?

No, he was too drunk to drive. Would he be mad at me if I wanted to leave? What would he say this time to make me feel stupid for asking?

Those were hard decisions to make for a girl of nine.

Yes, I would be brave. I would risk. I would ask to go to Gran's house.

Thankfully, Dad said I could go; Gran would come and get me and I'd go to her house, where I could also play with my good friend who lived near her.

I quickly packed my little cloth bag and ran outside to wait for Gran.

Once I got to Gran's house, my friend and I were invited to swim with a man many people admired and trusted.

Gran said it would be okay, so I got on my swimming suit, grabbed my beach towel, and headed for the lake.

The sky was getting dark, but I was familiar with the water and where the ladder was. My friend and I laughed as we jumped off the pier into the water. The man stayed in the water to catch us.

Over and over we jumped and came up the ladder to jump again. We were having such fun! For a while I forgot about my parents, their drinking, and what bad things happened in that house.

As I was going up the ladder again, something touched me where a little girl shouldn't be touched by a man. I knew the person touching me was the man we were with. It didn't feel good and it wasn't right.

At that moment the warm bubble of fun ended.

Not again! Not another man trying to hurt me!

I scrambled up the ladder, grabbed my towel, and ran down the pier to my Gran's house.

I ran so fast the water dried from my skin and my bathing suit stopped dripping. Inside the door, I ran right upstairs to my bedroom instead of stopping in the bathhouse to change out of my suit.

"How was the swim with your friends?" Gran called to me.

I couldn't tell her what had happened. Everyone liked this man. She wouldn't believe me. I would get in trouble if I told her the truth.

"Fine, Gran, but I'm cold and tired. I'm going to bed," I answered.

"Good night, sleep tight."

I climbed in bed and closed my eyes, but I couldn't forget what had just happened. I shivered every time I remembered the touch between my legs. I just wanted to have fun swimming and playing like the other girls.

Why did he do that to me? Why do boys and men keep trying to hurt me? What is wrong with me? Isn't there anywhere I can hide from people who want to do things to my body?

I slept some, but each time I woke up the dirty feelings were still there. And I didn't have any answers to my questions.

The next morning Gran had her yummy breakfast ready for me. I usually looked forward to her cooking, especially toast and her special spun honey.

But this morning I didn't feel like eating. My stomach felt jumpy.

I couldn't let Gran know what had happened to me the night before. She had said it was okay for me to swim with my friend and the older man. She couldn't have imagined that he had planned for more than just swimming with two young girls. I needed to leave before Gran asked any questions.

I gulped down as much breakfast as my queasy stomach could hold. When she gave me a puzzled look, I told her I wasn't very hungry. I hoped she would believe me.

I knew my dad would be there soon to pick me up. Once I got in the car, my dad wouldn't ask me anything; he probably wouldn't even talk to me. I could hide my feelings easily then.

I definitely could not tell him what happened. He would be angry with me. It would somehow be my fault.

The drive from Gran's house to my house wasn't very far. As I expected, the car was filled with silence. When we got home, Dad got out of the car, shut the door, and went inside the house.

I wasn't ready to go inside. I walked to my special hiding place where I could think.

When I had dressed at Gran's earlier that morning, I'd checked out the medicine cabinet of the upstairs bathroom. Sure enough, I'd found a new razor blade—the kind with two sharp edges. I'd tucked it in my bag before I went down for breakfast.

As I scurried toward my hiding place, I felt inside the bag. Yes, the razor blade was still there.

My safe hiding place wasn't far from my home. It was a cemetery—no one would look for me there.

I'd had a little sister, but she died at birth. I remember my mother staying in her bed for days crying about little Andrea Kay. I didn't see Mother cry over me or be very happy about me. I'd often wondered if she wished Andrea had lived and I had been the one who died.

I arrived at Andrea's grave with its little metal marker telling her name and the day she was born and died. A huge tombstone beside her grave marked where someone else was buried. I often went to the cemetery and hid behind that tombstone when I needed to get away from being hurt or wanted a place to cry where no one would see me. No one would look for me here.

As I crouched behind the tombstone, I devised a plan. My parents didn't want me. My family said I always caused trouble. My gran couldn't keep me safe from mean men.

I would make it better for me and for everyone. I would agree with my mom's words that I was bad and would never amount to anything. She said she wished I wasn't around. I would end my life. Everyone would be happy, and I wouldn't hurt anymore.

I reached in my bag for the razor blade. Ouch! It was sharp.

I touched it to my skinny wrist, pushed down a little, and slid the blade across my skin. A little red trickle came from the cut and ran down my arm.

I didn't go too deep the first time. I'd cut a little at a time.

I cut a thin line on my other wrist until I saw another trickle of red blood. It didn't hurt. I was so used to hiding pain. But the blood scared me. What was I going to do with all that blood? What if I weren't successful in killing myself and just made a big mess? Then I would really be in trouble.

Drip. Drip. Drip.

At first I felt numb as I watched the blood drip down my arm onto the ground. If I continued, more blood would be on the ground than in me and I'd be gone forever.

Did I really want to be gone forever?

I didn't know what being gone forever really meant, but it scared me. I didn't know what forever would be like. Would it be easier than the life I was living?

How does a little girl know the answers to these really hard questions?

Wait. What was that?

Something or someone got my attention. I couldn't see who it was, but I could feel its presence close by. Someone was there, and this time I didn't feel afraid. Who was it?

I felt warmth and peace surround me . . . and a bit of familiarity. I'd experienced other hard times when I was hurting badly and didn't think I had any way to escape the pain. I had felt this same presence some of those times.

Gran had told me about a person named Jesus who loved me
and was happy that I was alive. At night, when I visited there,
she read me Bible stories about this man and how He saved
little children who were in trouble.

Maybe what I felt near me was this Jesus. Maybe this Jesus
did want me. Would He hate me if I kept cutting myself? Would
He stop wanting me if I killed myself?

Did I really want to die? What if I just wanted someone to
see what was happening to me and make people stop hurting
me? Maybe He could stop them. Could I trust Him?

I didn't know much about trusting, especially trusting a man.

Someone I couldn't see with my earthly eyes in the graveyard
that day whispered that I should keep fighting to survive. I agreed.

I reached into my bag and took out a sock I had worn the
day before. I dabbed at the blood and held the white cloth over
the red lines until the bleeding stopped.

I didn't know very much about this Jesus—just a bit from
the stories Gran had read to me. In the stories things always
turned out good in the end. The children were always saved
from whatever trouble they had. Families always came quickly
to surround them with hugs and love. They were so glad the
little children were okay. They were happy they were alive.

I wasn't sure whether that could happen for me in my home
and neighborhood. But I felt sure this Jesus wanted me to keep
living. I couldn't explain it. It wouldn't make sense to anyone
else. But it made sense to me. It felt good to a lonely and confused little girl.

I slowly walked home, feeling I had a friend who wanted me
and would watch over me. He wouldn't keep all the bad things
from happening to me, but He would always be there to comfort

me. There would be more hard times and other stories of how His presence saved me.

Thankfully, I have sensed His presence and protection surrounding me many times as I've grown into an adult and throughout the journey of living.

Jesus Talked to Me

Agnes Lawless Weaver

"Agnes, I want you to be a missionary."

As a twelve-year-old girl, I stood rooted to the floor of my bedroom.

Did I hear a voice? It sounded like a voice. I didn't hear it with my ears but inside of me somehow.

A shiver went through me, and my heart pounded. *Maybe I'll hear it again. Maybe Jesus was talking to me. Dear Jesus, if that was you, will you please say it again?*

"Agnes, I want you to be a missionary."

You do? What should I do? Where should I go?

"I will be with you and will lead you."

I fell to my knees beside my bed. "O Lord, I'll go where you want me to go. I'll do what you want me to do. Thank you, Jesus, for talking to me!"

Peace filled my heart, for I felt that God had accepted my commitment. Then I became excited. *I need to tell Mother.*

I raced down the stairs and into the living room. "Mother!"

She was sitting by the window, darning a sock. She peered at me over her glasses and said, "Yes? What is it?"

"Jesus talked to me! He even called me by my name."

"You mean you heard His voice?"

"Yes, but it was inside of me. I didn't hear an actual voice."

She took another stitch. "What did He say?"

"He said He wants me to be a missionary!"

She looked at me over her glasses again and simply said, "Well, that's nice."

With those words, she burst my bubble of excitement.

How can she be so matter-of-fact, when this wonderful thing has happened? I thought. *I know she believes in missions, but maybe she thinks I'll soon forget it and get on with my life.*

But I didn't. I never forgot that voice and God's command. From then on, my goal in life was to get ready to become a missionary.

In my early years, we had lived in a large waterfront home on Bainbridge Island, Washington, with views of Mount Rainier and the Cascade Mountains. An efficient housekeeper we called "Nana" ran our home and cooked delicious meals. Mother was a professional vocalist who gave voice lessons and sang at weddings and funerals. We children played on the beach all summer, dove off our raft, and fished from our boat. It was an ideal life.

At the height of Dad's career, he won a contract with the U.S. government to put his deck machinery and whistles on all its ships. World War II was just around the corner, and this contract might have put him on top of the marine world.

But then a major eruption occurred in our family. At the age of fifty-four, Dad got pneumonia and died in four days, leaving

Mother with six children, ages four to seventeen. I was eight years old, next to the youngest.

With Dad's death, our world fell apart, and our entire family grieved. Night after night, I cried myself to sleep. I missed Daddy so much! And then my young friend next door died during an operation. What other terrible things would happen?

One day Mother kept my brother and me home from school because we were sick. She sewed and I read books, while my younger brother played with his toy cars.

As a fire in the fireplace crackled and snapped, we watched the wild waves chasing each other to shore.

But in that peaceful scene, my heart was heavy. I finally asked, "Mother, will I go to heaven when I die?"

"Yes, if you ask Jesus to come into your heart."

"How do I do that?"

I joined her on the sofa, where she told me more and led me in a short prayer: "Dear Jesus, please forgive me for my sins and come into my heart. I turn my life over to you."

Joy flooded my soul, and peace filled my worried mind. I soon loved reading my little Bible and praying to Jesus and my heavenly Father. I often shared the joy of my salvation with my young friends. Happily, two of them accepted Jesus as their Savior, too.

A year later, Mother sold our beautiful waterfront home and moved us to a small farm. It had an old two-story, white clapboard house and a large barn covered in cedar shakes. She planted a big vegetable garden, berry vines, and fruit trees. She also bought a cow, a sow, chickens, turkeys, and ducks. A friend gave us a beautiful collie puppy, mostly white with patches of brown. We named her Lassie. My younger brother and I loved that sweet dog. She comforted both of us and brought us joy.

And I continued to love and follow the Lord, even when an older sister needled me about my commitment to Christ.

When I was twelve, our church held a missions' conference. At a table in the back of the church, we looked at pictures and objects the missionaries had brought from the countries they'd served in. We sang songs with a missionary emphasis, such as "Send the Light" and "Bring Them In." Then we heard a missionary tell about his ministry among former headhunters in the mountains of Papua New Guinea.

I sat on the edge of my seat and listened. Since I had never heard a missionary speak before, I was moved by his stories of wild people turning their lives over to Christ and being transformed.

The next morning was when I heard Jesus' saying He wanted me to be a missionary.

I later attended a Christian high school where this fire in my heart was flamed. During a missions conference in my freshman year, I stood to indicate that I was dedicating my life to God for whatever He wanted me to do.

After I graduated from Bible college, I went to a Christian university and trained to be a teacher. While there, I became a leader in a foreign missions fellowship group. I learned that linguistic training would be helpful, so I attended a university offering a linguistic course taught by missionaries. During my two summers there, I joined Wycliffe Bible Translators.

Then I met and married a young man who was also a member, and we were assigned to the Philippines. He established a short-wave-radio network for our translators in remote locations.

Because I had had teachers' training, the director asked me to start a school for our young missionary children at our center on the southern island of Mindanao. I ordered supplies from the States and began to teach ten children in five grades. Our first schoolhouse was an old hut on stilts with a grass roof and a bamboo floor. Later, workmen built a real schoolhouse, and the number of students increased.

A few years later, I had surgery in a small clinic run by another mission. But my husband and I still had to return to the States to get more help. Full recovery took several years, so we resigned from the mission. I was devastated until a Christian doctor told me, "The field is the world."

But something good came out of not returning to the Philippines, for God opened other doors of mission—I started writing for publication and some of my books have been translated into other languages, so I have a much wider audience than I ever had before and can minister in places I don't visit anymore.

And it all began when I heard God's voice in that old farmhouse.

Mattie's Angel

Joann Claypoole

My five-year-old son, Matthew, and I accompanied my father while he went to the doctor. Now the fresh diagnosis, "lung cancer," haunted our drive home and melted any thought of our stopping by the local ice cream shop on the way.

My head pounded. My heart ached. I gripped the steering wheel and prayed, *God, please help him—please. I love him.*

I hoped I'd wake up. But it wasn't a dream.

Dad had only a few weeks to live.

Tears streamed down my face, and my normally happy heart felt empty. A thousand thoughts swarmed in my mind. One rang the loudest: *Lord, please be with the children while we're in this valley.*

Only one sentence broke my silence. It fell out of my mouth as if I, too, were a child again. "Daddy . . . please don't leave me."

"Come on now, no more tears." He handed me a tissue and winked. "You know where I'm going."

Matthew sat in the backseat. His head was bowed and hands pressed together. "But where are you going, Poppy? I thought you liked it here."

I looked at my youngest son through the rearview mirror. *He loves his grandfather. How am I going to tell him?* I managed a coherent answer. "Mattie, Poppy's sick. We need to say lots of prayers for him."

He looked up for a moment. His brown eyes widened. "I bet some chocolate ice cream would have made him feel better."

"Not today, Matt."

"Don't worry, Mom. You always say we have guardian angels watching over us. Dad says we have a hedge of them around our house every night. Maybe Poppy's angel is tired and forgot to do his job."

I kept one hand on the steering wheel and reached the other out to my father.

The unwavering strength of his voice soothed my weary heart. "No, Matthew, he didn't forget. God's angels are *His* helpers. They're always watching over us in accordance with *His* plan for our lives—even when it looks like they forgot to do their job."

Matt sighed. "I don't get it. But I'm sure God hears Mom singing songs to Him all the time. He won't forget us."

We moved my father into our home later that day. I read psalms and sang to him every morning. My three sons sat on his bed after school and listened to his war stories. My husband played cards with him at night. Priceless moments of unexplainable peace in the midst of this storm filled us during the two weeks that followed.

Early one morning, Matthew walked into the kitchen after his two older brothers had left for school, telling me about an experience he and one of his brothers had.

"Cliff and I watched Poppy lift his arms up toward the ceiling. We heard him whispering—Cliff said he wasn't speaking to us. Poppy waved, pointed at the bedroom door, and then he told Cliff to sit on the bed. 'You're blocking my view of the angel behind you,' he said to us. We both turned to look—but we didn't see it."

I set my coffee cup on the counter and smiled for the first time in two weeks. A rush of warmth filled me. Hundreds of tiny goose bumps raised on my arms. I didn't understand why I felt comforted, but I welcomed this odd reassurance as a sweet sign from heaven.

Matthew skipped across the tile floor and began to giggle. "Poppy said it smiled at us—and it looked like Cliff! I asked if my angel visited him, but he said, 'Not yet.' I wonder what he—I mean *it*—looks like?"

I scooped him up and kissed his forehead. "Of course *it* smiled at you. You're the cutest five-year-old on earth!"

Later that evening, my father's restlessness settled. I managed to slip away from my constant bedside vigil to snuggle with my boys during our evening prayer time. I tucked Mattie's covers around him, kissed all the boys good night, cleaned the kitchen, and finally dragged myself to bed at midnight.

The sudden thumping of someone running toward our bedroom at 3:00 a.m. startled my husband and me. We threw our tangled sheets to the floor and bolted toward the children's rooms.

Trembling, Matthew met us in the hallway. He leapt into his daddy's arms.

"I couldn't sleep. I finally prayed and asked God to take care of Poppy if He decides to take him home to heaven. I told Him I'm sure Mom would like to know her daddy will be okay. I also asked Him to help me believe it, too. Then I heard a low swooshing sound. I opened one eye, peeked out from my covers, and—"

Mattie pointed to his bedroom doorway. "*He* stood right there. I thought it was Dad—then his wings started to flap. The hallway lit up with an orange glow. He wore a whitish-gold robe. I pulled my blanket up over my head, shut my eyes tight, and yelled for Mom. That's when my angel disappeared. And I ran."

My heart leapt. "It had to be a dream," I said.

But my heart already believed something amazing had happened in our home. My precious boy's innocent heart moved my spirit to believe in those miraculous moments.

"He was here," Matt insisted. "And I want to name him James."

God, your angels really are here with us. Thank you, Lord.

Matthew hugged me tightly.

"I love you, Mommy," he said and yawned.

We said our third round of prayers, and his dad tucked Matt in again.

As we walked out of his room, he squealed, "Mommy, I think Poppy asked my angel to come for a visit. What do you think?"

I laughed. "I think you're my favorite five-year-old. Love you. Now go to sleep, sweetie."

Peace enveloped me the rest of the night and all the next day. The following evening I held my father's hand when he passed away.

At his memorial service, I reached into my purse for a tissue but pulled out a piece of paper, a note written by my dad on the same day I had taken him to the doctor.

I smiled and read: "Thank you. Love always, Dad."

My tears flowed as I stared at my first hero's last written words.

Now, eighteen years later, my three sons, and especially twenty-three-year-old Matthew, still remember him fondly—and Mattie's story about his angel, James, remains the same to this day.

Matt recently said, "I remember saying the angel looked like Dad. The funny thing is, now that I'm an adult, I think he looked like me."

My father always believed love never fails. "God's love is always with you," he'd said. "It will carry you through life's valleys and strengthen you along the way—and His angels will always be near to watch over you every day."

"Even when I walk through the darkest valley, I will not be afraid, for you are close beside me" (Psalm 23:4).

A Visit From the Healer

Dawn Aldrich

As I answered the phone, fear pierced my heart. My baby girl was perched on my hip while her brother and a few day-care kids played in the next room. I held the phone to my ear and listened while my husband's angry words roared above the toddlers' playfulness. He had lost his job.

I leaned against the kitchen wall and searched for the right response. But no words formed.

Questions swirled through my mind.

Will we be okay? Will he find another job? How will we pay the bills? Will we have to sell the house? What about health insurance?

You know the questions you have when a scenario you hope will never happen suddenly happens.

As I hung up the phone, I plastered a brave face over my tears for my kids' sakes.

In the following weeks, our hope increased with every odd job and new day-care client, but so did our unpaid bills. We prayed harder and eliminated life's luxuries like date nights, cable TV, newspaper delivery, commercial garbage pick-up, and health insurance.

We believed miracles happened all the time, but we couldn't see ours anywhere. In fact, the more we prayed and the more we sacrificed, the more distant God seemed—until our faith teetered on disbelief.

One night I sat rocking our inconsolable baby girl while she communicated that a searing pain shot through her left ear. On top of stressing about the prolonged unemployment, a hefty mortgage, and unpaid bills, this was the last straw. This mama's heart just couldn't take any more. When it came to my own pain, I could tolerate almost anything, but I couldn't watch my writhing baby girl.

Laying my screaming baby in her crib, I frantically prayed on my way to the medicine cabinet for Tylenol. "Jesus, if you're really here, if you're really listening, please, help us! We simply can't afford a doctor's visit. Please help!"

Armed with a dropper of cherry-flavored relief, I stopped outside the nursery door. Instead of screams and tears I heard coos and gibbering, then laughing and jumping.

What was going on in there? Who was she talking to? Maybe someone had slipped into her room when my back was turned.

I crept inside and looked around, but no one was there except my baby girl, smiling like the Cheshire cat in *Alice in Wonderland*.

"He fixed it, Mommy!" She beamed, jumping up and down in her crib.

"Who fixed what?" I asked.

"My ear. He fixed my ear!" she repeated in her toddler language, pointing to her bookcase lined with stuffed animals and dolls.

"Who fixed your ear, honey?"

"He did!"

Pointing to her overstuffed collections, I started the interrogation. "Did Teddy fix your ear?"

"No," she replied.

"Did Bunny, or Bert, or Ernie fix your ear?"

"No, no, no!" She giggled a second, third, and fourth time. "*He* fixed my ear!" she exclaimed, indignantly pointing to her bookcase.

Still treating the idea of a miracle coolly, I played along. "Does this man have big wings? Is he an angel? Did an angel fix your ear?"

"No, Mommy. *He* fixed my ear."

How would she know the difference between an angel and a man, anyway? I scoffed to myself.

Then one of her board books, *Jesus and the Children*, caught my eye. It was her favorite bedtime story, and we must have read it to her hundreds of times, including that night.

Holding it up, I turned to the picture of Jesus playing leapfrog with the children and asked: "Did *He* fix your ear? Did Jesus touch your ear?"

"Yes."

"*Jesus* fixed your ear? He *did*?"

"Yes."

I choked back tears and whispered one more question, "Is Jesus *still* here?"

"Yes," she replied calmly and pointed over my shoulder.

Chills shivered down my neck, but not fearful chills. These chills signified something different—something miraculous—when heaven meets earth in one split second.

Jesus was here! He was physically present in my house—listening, caring, and performing miracles all around me—but I couldn't see Him. My daughter could see what I couldn't, perhaps because she didn't wear spiritual blinders like I did.

My daughter snuggled beneath her covers and fell fast asleep. I left her room pondering, thinking this might be some cruel joke.

I expected her pain to return the next day. But I awoke the next morning reassured that not only was Jesus our *Jehovah Rapha* (the God who heals) but He was also our *Jehovah Jireh* (the God who provides).

Slowly through the next few months, my spiritual blinders fell loose. Not that I could physically see Jesus moving, but I knew from then on, He was ever present and everything would be okay.

More than twenty years have passed since that night, and my daughter never experienced another earache. There is no human explanation for how I left my daughter screaming in pain one minute and, without the aid of medicine, found her laughing, jumping, chattering, and pain-free moments later. Jesus is the only explanation.

My husband found work months later through people only Jesus could have placed in our lives, and through God's grace and provision we kept our home. Life moved forward, and when tough times hit again—whether we needed physical, emotional, or financial help—God reminded us of His faithfulness on that night long ago.

Do miracles really happen? Yes. Miracles happen every day. Expect them.

Hope Beyond the Smoke

Julie B. Cosgrove

The weather matched my mood on that overcast, cold evening a few days after Christmas the year I was thirteen. My parents had gone to a society function, as they often did because my father was in politics. Since I was a young teen, they felt I could be left alone in the house without supervision.

That year had been a horrible year of loss for me. My brother married, my sister went off to college, and my mother went back to school to get her master's degree in speech pathology.

We'd sold the home I'd grown up in and moved across town to an apartment complex away from all my best friends.

I left the eleven-year-old cat I'd cherished most of my life behind at the house. She was almost blind, and my parents felt it would be better if she were in familiar surroundings. The new owners promised they would care for her.

That didn't happen. She escaped after days of howling as she searched for me and was hit by a car.

Besides all that, I began to wade in the teenage hormonal waves that loomed and threatened to engulf me. This added up to one depressed, borderline-suicidal girl.

That Christmas I received a Tensor lamp—the latest cool gizmo—from my parents. It had a crane-like neck that could bend in any direction and clip onto the headboard so I could read into the wee hours, which I often did. It had a high-intensity bulb with a hard-to-miss warning sticker: "Do not touch. HOT."

That night when my parents were out, I fell asleep reading. I was sound asleep when the lamp unclipped and fell onto the mattress. The fibers began to smolder from the intense heat. In my sleep, I felt hot and my throat became scratchy.

It's okay. You're coming down with something. Sleep. There's nothing worth getting up for, my inner voice assured.

Like a clap of thunder, another booming voice of authority pierced my subconscious. *"Julie. Get up. Now!"*

I bolted awake in a smoke-engulfed room. I couldn't see a thing. Then, in an instant, the smoke parted and I saw the door swing open. But I was alone, wasn't I?

The outdoor security floodlight streamed into the hallway from the sliding glass door off my parents' master bedroom—it was the beacon to safety I needed.

"Go!" the voice commanded.

I stumbled to the sliding door and opened it. I couldn't get enough air into my lungs to scream. I collapsed onto the third floor balcony, the billowing smoke cloaking me.

I vaguely remember some strangers shouting. I watched as they tossed my mattress off the balcony to the apartment drive-way below. In midair, it burst into flames. Pieces floated down like illuminated confetti.

The next thing I recall, I was lying on the couch, breathing through an oxygen mask and peering at my mother. Medical professionals hovered nearby. I heard the scratchy caw of their walkie-talkies. Then everything filtered into darkness.

My parents said I slept for most of the day. I awoke in the middle of the night calling their names. After they hugged me and re-tucked me into the guest bed, they returned to their own room.

But I couldn't sleep. I lay there staring at the ceiling. The pungency of smoke still lingered in my nose. I began to process what had happened. The reality of how close to death I'd come slapped me in the face. My heart caught in my throat and tears filled my eyes.

I slid onto my knees and whispered, "God . . . that was you who divided the smoke and opened the door, right? You led me to the balcony."

I sucked in a breath of clean, sweet air. The tears in my eyes cascaded down my face, unabashed, like a cleansing shower. I reached up my hands, fingers spread. In between sobs I prayed. "I didn't think my life was worth anything, but you must. You saved me. So I give it to you. Tell me what to do with it."

We were not big churchgoers. I had no idea what I'd just done. I didn't know about being reborn. But I began to read the Bible and asked to go to church. A youth minister took me under his wing, and I eventually accepted Christ as my Savior.

He has never let go of me since that day. I know He let me live so I can tell others of His mercy and grace. If you know of someone who is struggling with whether or not to keep on living, I hope you will share this story with him or her. God loves that person just as much as He loves you and me. There is hope beyond the smoke.

His Name Is Enough

Dianne Fraser

My early teen years were filled with uncertainty and anxiety that went beyond the normal puberty experience. After the safe haven of elementary school, I was tipped out of my comfortable environment and catapulted into junior high school.

The adjustment wasn't just difficult; it was intolerable. My first day of class, I was so terrified I thought I might faint. I had none of the social skills required for making friends, so I tried to keep out of sight as much as possible and felt physically sick. I was the perfect fodder for a bit of fun at the hands of the more confident students.

The harassment started with name-calling. I endured names, labels, having my physical faults highlighted and mocked, and being left on my own, never being picked for teams. The emotional damage was severe and immense.

Then the taunting began to get physical at times as I was pushed around and threatened. The abuse was subtle enough that the perpetrators were never caught, and it was always done in ways that would make it hard for me to make a case against anyone. While the girls did these things, the boys played other games. They sat next to me on the school bus and made lurid comments about what they would like to do with me. They would snigger at the game I was unwittingly part of. Each would try to outdo the last and then share their expressed intents with one another.

That, of course, led to my being labeled as something I wasn't.

The shame and sense of worthlessness began to build—but I would hold it all together until my head hit the pillow at night. Then I cried myself to sleep.

I know I should have spoken up and talked to my wonderful parents or a teacher. But I had no courage or self-confidence to do so. The bullies said if I made trouble, they would double their efforts. That kept me silent.

I began to develop tools to protect myself—one was not to eat or drink during school hours. This had a twofold benefit. First, I could spend more time in the library. As soon as the lunch bell rang, I was lining up for the library instead of gathering with others to have my lunch.

Nobody bothered me in the library, and it was the only place I felt any sense of safety. I could protect myself from the taunts and stares and mocking and pretend that I was okay.

Second, if I didn't eat or drink, I could better avoid the restrooms, where I was in danger of having my head flushed in the toilet bowl. One encounter with that humiliation was enough to make me stay away from even a remote possibility of that happening again.

This was my world—filled with a deep ache, immense fears, and loneliness that followed me everywhere.

My mum was a deeply spiritual woman who lived her faith as a reality. In her mind, which flowed into her actions, no wound was too big for God to heal, and no issue was too great for Him to solve.

This was a message she often repeated—that when facing anxiety or fears, I should call on Jesus' name. She believed if we whisper His name over and over amid turmoil, we'll find an awareness of His presence—and that this nearness will bring calm.

I had heard this a hundred times, but I hadn't really considered doing it.

I clearly recall one very hot day at school. Not drinking had physical consequences of dehydration at the best of times, but this day, I knew I would have to endure the humiliation of fainting if I didn't visit the water fountain. That water tasted great as I drank deep. But it led to a different kind of humiliation.

As the final bell sounded for the day, I had to run for the bus. Full of water, my bladder was aching for a bathroom break. However, my fear of the tough crowd who inhabited the girls' restroom was too great.

I stepped onto the bus for the half-hour trip home, deeply afraid of the unimaginably shameful occurring.

Just before we arrived at my stop, my bladder could hold no more, and I felt the warm rush of urine staining my uniform. I was a thirteen-year-old girl experiencing what no teen should.

I worked hard to hold the tears, knowing I would never exit the bus without being noticed if I showed any emotion. I had learned the necessity of being invisible in order to survive.

I was so relieved when I stepped off the bus, shielding myself with my school sweater and book bag, and no one seeming to know.

My brothers were both sick that day, so I began the short walk up the gravel road toward the farm blessedly on my own. As I walked, I could smell the urine, and my body began to heave. I sat under a tree on the roadside and let the tears and shame break free.

And I whispered Jesus' name.

Then I whispered it again. Desperate. Pleading. Needing someone to see me and know me and love me.

At a point of complete solitude and brokenness, I called out to the Savior, and my life changed in that moment.

As I whispered His name through my tears a third time, peace stole into my heart. This thirteen-year-old girl who didn't believe anything good could come of her life found herself in God's presence.

I cried as I continued to whisper His name. As the tears fell and the pain bubbled up from inside, I knew I was not alone. I was sitting under a tree with the Savior. He was there beside me. He was there in my heart—soothing, calming, giving peace that I now know can only be attributed to the eternal, sovereign, all-knowing Creator.

The real change continued for me. I believed He was there in the empty chair next to me in the classroom. The lonely corner of the library became a place where I could share my heart with Him. The bus ride home became an opportunity to gaze out the window and speak to my ever-present Helper. As my confidence grew in Him, confidence grew in me. Life began to change.

It took only a whisper to beckon Him. But it was a whisper that allowed me to sense the reality and presence of God, as real as anything I can see.

Jesus. It is truly the name that changes lives.

He Floated in Front of the Cross

Judith Victoria Hensley

As a child, I was sure I heard the voices of angels worshiping God in the melody of babbling brooks that ran across my parents' mountain property. I sometimes thought I saw those angels sitting in the tree branches among the dogwoods in spring.

I even heard the heavenly choir lifting praises to God in the majesty of a sunset. I was certain the whippoorwill and the bobolink were conducting their evening vespers to God when their lonesome calls sounded.

These things were normal to me. I thought everyone's heart belonged to God and beat in harmony with the vast creation that worshiped Him.

I was surprised when I first found out that others were skeptical that I'd seen or heard anything heavenly. And I was shocked when I discovered that others could not see or hear those things that were so precious to me. Whether it was through the doubt of others or the transition of growing older, my commune with God through nature vanished from my life.

However, my faith in God never faltered. My belief that He cared for me as an individual and my firm conviction that God constantly communicates with those who pay attention never diminished. But years passed before I saw or heard anything else of a spiritual nature that was unusual.

Every August our church sent the teen group to a week of youth camp in Manteno, Illinois. We looked forward to it from one year to the next. We exchanged letters with our youth camp friends through the winter months and counted down the calendar until we would all be one big happy family again for that one week of August. It was an amazing adventure for so many teenagers to worship and learn about God together. It was like a bit of heaven coming down just for us.

One summer a special event was scheduled for the last evening of camp: an outdoor drama of the story of Christ's life called *The Crucifixion*. We didn't have to memorize a script. The presentation was recorded and would be played over speakers outdoors. We only had to walk through the motions in costume, remember our cues, and flow with the prerecorded recitation and musical score.

I played one of the women at the foot of the cross. As we practiced, I felt chills as I thought of what it would have been like to be there when Jesus Christ was nailed to a cross, wounded and bloody.

What agony must have been felt as the women and men who loved Him watched Him die. The disappointment, fear, and lack of understanding must have been devastating. I entered that world each time we practiced.

147

The week progressed as usual with meals in the mess hall, morning Bible classes, afternoon activities like softball and volleyball, and nightly services. In between we practiced walking through *The Crucifixion*.

On the last evening, the area we would use for our performance was roped off. The audience would watch from a hillside, looking onto the field where the action would take place. As church groups, pastors, and parents began to show up for the performance, I felt a holy reverence in the air.

From the moment the soundtrack began to play, amplified through the trees, across the field, and up the hillside, something was different about it. Perhaps the volume was turned up higher than it had been all week. Possibly the hundreds of pairs of eyes trained on us heightened our awareness. Whatever was going on felt very different from our rehearsals.

When we reached the crucifixion scene, the cat-o'-nine-tails that was used to whip Jesus across His back had been stained with red food coloring so that it looked like blood streaking from the actor's body. The thud of iron on wood as they simulated nailing the spikes through His hands was bone jarring and heartrending.

By the end of the presentation, people were breaking through the ropes and coming forward at the invitation to ask Jesus Christ into their lives and to give their hearts to God. They pressed in around me as I kneeled on the ground before an empty cross. I had never before seen such an emotional response from a crowd.

Eventually the emotion subsided, the service broke up, and people were chatting as they left the performance field. Some stragglers stayed behind longer to pray or talk with one another on the lawn.

But a small group of us could not leave. Still in costume, still on our knees before an empty cross, we could not leave that holy place.

As I knelt there, I poured my heart out to God. I wanted Him to know how much I loved Him. I wanted Jesus to know that I realized His suffering and sacrifice were for me. I wanted my life to count for God's kingdom.

As a teenager, I had no worldly goods to give, no riches to lay down at His feet. I had nothing to offer Him except my love, my heart, myself. I wanted God to accept the gift of my life, a gift I offered of my own free will.

His presence was so real that He seemed to walk among the dozen or so who had stayed behind, and we could not end the connection so easily. He was so real, I was afraid to look up, afraid of what I might see, yet compelled to look at the same time.

When I raised my head, I saw Him there, in white robes, shining in the waning light. He was literally floating in front of the cross, His hands reaching toward us. The love was palpable.

I looked at the others who remained. Some of them were also looking in the direction where I saw the figure. We all seemed to be suspended for a moment outside of time.

I heard no audible voice, but I heard His message in my heart: "Many are called, but few are chosen. . . . I am with you always, even to the end of the age" (Matthew 22:14; 28:20 NLT).

When the figure disappeared, the sound of sobbing renewed briefly, and almost on cue we stood.

We all knew something incredible, a true spiritual encounter, had taken place and we had shared it, but no one talked about it. I don't know if they shared it with their friends or family. I tried to, but just as I had learned as a child, if others don't see or hear what you have seen and heard, they can't understand it or grasp it as real.

Through the years I have thought of those who knelt in the grass that day. I've wondered if they spent their lives serving the Lord. I did find out years later that several were in the ministry. Perhaps they received their calling that night.

I am not sure that I've ever accomplished any grand thing, but I have tried to serve the Lord in everything I do, one day at a time.

I listen for His voice and am assured that He still speaks to His children, and that all of nature declares His glory. The brooks still sing their songs to Him. Creation still declares His glory. Angel choirs still praise Him. And the most I have to offer Him is my heart, my love, my life—all of me.

A Very Special Easter

Lynnette Goldy

At twelve years old, wearing a white dress, matching hat and gloves, black patent leather shoes, and sitting in the sanctuary with my parents and sisters, I felt a bit pale.

Will I feel the change immediately? Will it take time? Will it be a one-time deal?

I had so many unanswered questions. And I was nervous.

This was a very special Easter. I was looking forward to my baptism. I thought I understood what happens during a baptism. I would, in a sense, die and then I would be reborn with Christ.

I had accepted Christ as my Savior and knew I wanted to spend the rest of my life with Him. I didn't know what that picture would look like. But I knew my baptism was going to help paint that picture.

Finally, the pastor called me up front and the deaconess guided me behind the baptistery. She led me to a little room and gave me a white robe to change into.

Despite being covered, I felt naked. Exposed. A bit embarrassed. What happened to that pretty picture I was painting just a few minutes ago?

I knew the routine. I had watched my older sister's baptism a few years earlier, and she didn't seem any different. But I knew I was already different. I could feel it. I wondered if putting on the robe was like putting on Christ.

We had attended classes where the pastor explained what happens during baptism. We would be asked some questions and then lowered three times into the water—in the name of the Father, in the name of the Son, and in the name of the Holy Spirit. Our sins would be forgiven and we would start a new life. We would begin living our eternal life.

Instead of being born once and dying twice, we would be born twice and die once. I liked that.

I also liked the privileges that baptism would bring. A few months earlier, I had asked my mother if I could borrow a dish towel from our kitchen. I used it to cover the end table next to the couch in our basement. I would sometimes go to the basement because I could be alone there with Jesus. I placed on the table a cross and a picture of Jesus. I set out a little plate of crackers and a glass of grape juice and offered myself Communion. *This is the body and blood of Jesus. Do this in remembrance of me* (see Luke 22:19).

I could hardly wait to be baptized and take real Communion. And today was the day.

A couple of my friends were also being baptized. From my dressing room I heard the water splash against the sides of the baptistery as the first one got in. I heard the pastor's voice but not his exact words. I heard the water splash and the pastor's voice again.

And then I heard the whole thing happen again a second and third time with other friends.

Then my name was called.

It's my turn. Lord, forgive me all my sins and help me live my life for you, I prayed.

The deaconess took my arm so I wouldn't slip on the water on the floor. I walked down the steps alone into the baptistery.

And then it was over. I had been dunked three times as I held my nose. The pastor said the words.

Something happened that I can't explain. I didn't really do anything but answer the questions and go under the water. But I'll never forget that moment. I was a different person through the miracle of baptism.

I truly felt I had been reborn.

I got dressed and went back to the sanctuary to join my family. Everyone was clapping!

The tray of crackers was passed. I took one and looked at it in my hand. I placed it in my mouth as the pastor said, "This is the body of Christ."

The tray of grape juice came by. I took a cup.

"This is the blood of Christ."

I heard Jesus' words. I heard the Word of God.

Not long before, I had taken Communion in my basement—just me and God. Now I was taking it with the entire congregation, and I still felt like it was just God and me.

Is that what baptism does? Does baptism make Communion feel more personal?

I know I am part of the family of God now. I feel closer to everyone around me because of my baptism. But I also feel closer to God than I did before. Surely God is with me.

After church we went to my grandparents' house for Easter dinner as we always did. All the kids brought playclothes to change into as we normally did. We all sat around the table as we always had. We ate ham and scalloped potatoes and Jell-O salad and all the usual food.

The adults talked as they normally did. And after dinner the kids spent the better part of the afternoon outside while some of the adults napped. So far, nothing seemed to have changed since my baptism. I was glad.

I had hoped this feeling I had of a new life would last forever. The feeling has ebbed and flowed, but the fact that I am living a new life has remained. God did His part in my baptism, and I need to live my life for Him the best I can.

I've made some major mistakes and a lot of little ones, too. But I also know that when I ask, God forgives me. He is with me every step of the way as I continue to paint the picture of my life one brushstroke at a time.

I choose what colors to use. It's my choice the landscape I paint. The path I take is my choice. But I have chosen to paint my life with Christ's paintbrush.

I have changed and I continue to change, for the better. How do I know it's for the better? Because I have accepted Christ as my Savior and I still pursue Him. Life is not all roses. I continue to struggle to live the Christian life. It is an ongoing process of repentance and forgiveness, of falling and getting back up. But I keep remembering that very special Easter, so many years ago.

The Black Hag From Hell

Kate Barrows

Living through the Illinois winters had brought me to my limit. After finishing high school, I went to Bethel School of Supernatural Ministry in Redding, California. One of my sisters had moved there with her husband and two kids and attended a charismatic church that people from all over the world had come to. I joined her and learned about the spiritual gifts, including prophecy, healing, and demonic deliverance—the latter would come in quite handy down the road.

After the academic year in California was over, I spent some time in Texas with my brother and sister-in-law, looking after their two beautiful little boys. Then I decided to return to Illinois for a job at Starbucks—my first full-time retail job in the real world.

Over the months I mastered the task of making dozens of coffee combinations in short order. Courses at the local community college rounded out my daily routine and kept me contentedly busy and occasionally exhausted.

I took walks along the Prairie Path near my home and enjoyed kicking the freshly fallen leaves in the cool breeze and spotting the occasional deer in the distance.

But the crisp, bright autumn suddenly turned into the cruelest winter Chicago had experienced in twenty years. There were twenty-three sub-zero days, and that didn't even take into consideration the wind-chill factor—not to mention the days where the temperature climbed only into the single digits.

The sun didn't appear for weeks, or so it seemed, and every few days we would get a light snowfall to pile onto the existing mass of dirty snow and slush. I had little to do in my spare time but work out at my local fitness center or watch another video in my friend's basement.

February 17 turned out to be a fateful day. I was stir-crazy and just wanted to get out of the house. I told my dad I would pick up my paycheck, and as he looked out at the unplowed street, he reminded me to put the SUV into four-wheel drive.

So off I went over the snow-covered roads to my workplace, and then with check in hand climbed into my vehicle, thankful that I had the protection of what seemed like an armored car.

As I pulled out onto the main highway, however, a semitruck came barreling down the center lane.

I prudently merged back into the right lane and picked up speed.

Suddenly the truck driver made a quick move into my lane and it looked like his tail would knock me off the road.

I slammed on the brakes. My SUV spun out of control. The rest was a blur.

The next thing I knew, I was hanging upside down and a fireman was breaking the window. An eyewitness saw my vehicle flip three times; my dad later took a picture of it facing backward, the high beams reflecting off the snow on the side of the road. In my shock, I called my dad, but told him I didn't want to interfere with his evening. I told him I could get a ride home with a co-worker. But knowing the SUV was out of commission made him realize he'd better get to the accident scene immediately.

A band of angels must have protected me, as I was perfectly fine. But believe me, it was enough to make me want to return to sunny California again—this time for a long time!

My chance came four months later, when a position opened up at a Starbucks close to the beach in southern Los Angeles. I packed my bags and headed out for the second time, hoping the year-round beautiful weather, miles of pristine beaches, hip culture, and my sister's family close by would keep me there for a long time. I would live with the same great roommate, as well, from my Bethel School of Supernatural Ministry days in Redding.

Things got off to a slow start, with the usual challenges of finding enough work hours, paying the bills, getting the basics for my room, and so forth. But I was happy to be in this promising part of the country and working up to eventually doing what I had always dreamed of. Little did I know the most harrowing experience of my life was just around the corner.

After a number of months of working without much of a break, I was delighted when my sister invited my roommate (who was her children's nanny) and me to join her at a very posh place up the California coast where she would sometimes go to relax. The owners were special friends of hers and had made the place available for the weekend.

The house was built by a famous architect at the turn of the last century and was like a stone castle set on the side of a cliff, looking down to the bay with sea otters floating in the sun, and the roaring ocean waves just beyond.

When we learned that we would be staying in another building on the property, about a hundred yards from the house, my roommate and I were intrigued. It was a combination greenhouse and living quarters built in the round, enclosed in polished redwood and with lots of windows. There was the greenhouse level and another with two small bedrooms.

As we settled down for the night in our rooms, I could hear the sound of the waves crashing on the rocks far below. I decided to keep my door open for the soothing sound.

But as I fell into a deep sleep, I was accosted by a vivid dream. I heard a sharp gunshot and saw ahead of me the figure of a man looking at me with an evil sneer and a bullet hole in the middle of his forehead.

I jolted awake. The darkness around me was filled with a sense of dread. We all have occasional bad dreams, but the atmosphere was dark and heavy beyond the physical darkness.

The next night my subconscious was on guard against any kind of spiritual attack. I was lying in bed in the dark, very much awake, both vigilant and wanting to sleep at the same time.

For some reason, I left my door open again for the soothing sound and pleasant night air. The moon was clear, illuminating the cliff.

And then I not only saw it clearly, but heard it plainly as well. I pulled my covers up, sitting up slightly in bed. A jet-black being with a paper-thin body that seemed to wave in the wind at the open door made a shrill, blood-curdling wail. Its hair was freaky—long and willowy, slithering like individual snakes from its head, like Medusa from Greek mythology.

Worse, it was slowly coming toward me with a gaze of evil intent, shrieking as it came.

Soon it would be upon me and surely try to suck the life out of me.

Suddenly my training in demonic deliverance thrust to the front of my mind. As the black spirit "hag" tried to come upon me, I commanded it in the name of Jesus, by His victory on the cross over the forces of evil, to be gone. It lifted up but then seemed to lie down beside me, wailing. I continued to invoke the blood of Jesus and the armor of God.

Whatever it was quieted and floated out into the moonlit night.

I was shaking and sweating and my heart was pounding, so I tiptoed out of the room and into the room where my roommate was sleeping. I continued to pray and thank God that He had delivered me from such a tangible presence of evil.

The next morning I described the experience to my sister, who agreed that I had come in contact with a demon. It was a vivid reminder to me that God is always with me, just as He was when my SUV rolled and I exited without a scratch.

We need not fear or be surprised when we are confronted with evil, but use the authority God has given us to resist it in Jesus' name.

My Angel Watching My Heart

Marie Weaver

"Surgery has been scheduled for September first."

At the words from my son's pediatric cardiologist, anxiety raced through my mind and heart. My husband, Don, and I thought we were ready to hear them. But we weren't. Who would be?

Since the day Sean was born, I had prayed daily that his life would please God, that God would care for him and provide me with the skills to help him grow strong and healthy.

Sean endured so much during his first two years of life. He was only eight days old when he had his first surgery. Then our biweekly trips to either the cardiologist or the pediatrician took a lot of time and wore him out. His little body was poked, weighed, measured, and tested until he didn't want anyone to bother him. The doctor listened to his tiny, deformed, overworked heart. We discussed his eating habits, lack of weight gain, physical ability and limitations, and general activity levels. I was tired of it all, too.

Of course, Sean didn't understand that all the medicine, the tests, and the tears were leading up to the surgery that would hopefully save his life.

I continually prayed over his young life to the God of love, the God who promises compassion and peace no matter how difficult life is. I often praised God for His promise "Praise be to the God and Father of our Lord Jesus Christ, the Father of compassion and the God of all comfort" (2 Corinthians 1:3).

And I wondered what kind of healing God would provide. I intended to trust God for all He would give.

The day before Sean's open-heart surgery was filled with tears and tests. Sean screamed when blood was drawn from his aching hands. I held him as closely as possible, praying that God would hold him tighter than I could and ease the pain. I continued to pray, asking God to give us all peace.

"God, I know deep in my heart that this is your plan for healing!" I whispered.

Early the next morning the doctors and nurses prepared Sean for his surgery, and I prayed that all would go well.

As we walked into the operating room, Sean's body tensed and a few tears gathered in his eyes. He was scared. As I handed him to the surgeon and nurse, I silently begged God to comfort Sean.

The doctor said he would let us know when the procedure was complete.

In the waiting room I saw many other worried parents. I felt God's arms wrap around my shoulders, holding me with His strength and a sense of peace. I wondered if any of them felt it, too.

Meanwhile, a few complications set in for Sean. His heart wasn't responding well to the surgeon's corrections. It took time to fix the issues, to get Sean's heart to beat properly on its own. They told me later it was touch and go for a while.

After several hours we learned that Sean's surgery was a success. God's answer to Sean's physical healing was at hand.

Years later, when Sean was about five years old, he told me about his day of surgery.

"Mom, your friend Jean looks like the angel that held my hand when I had my heart operation," he said.

"When you had your open-heart surgery? You remember that time? You were just two years old."

"Yes, I saw myself on that table with the doctor and nurses standing around it. But someone was holding my hand. She looked like your friend." He continued, "She was pretty. I felt warm and I wasn't scared. She was with me all the time. Do you think she was an angel?"

In my prayer time that day I read Psalm 91:11: "For he will command his angels concerning you to guard you in all your ways."

God had fulfilled this Scripture with Sean! Hallelujah!

I said a silent prayer of thanks for God's special helper. While Sean was having surgery and I was in the waiting room, I knew that God was watching over him, healing his little body. But I hadn't known that God had sent a special angel and that Sean saw the angel and could remember how she looked years later.

While God was taking care of Sean's heart, He was also taking care of his soul.

Today Sean is almost thirty years old. He hasn't seen the angel since that day, yet he still remembers and can describe her. When he talks about her, his face glows, his eyes twinkle, and I know that he remembers the warmth and love he felt. Sean has a special bond with God because of that experience.

He tells me that because of what happened then, he lives one day at a time, thanking God. He believes that no matter the obstacles of his life, God is watching over him and providing for him.

When I pray, I expect God to answer. He may hold me in His arms. He may send a special messenger or angel of comfort. But He *will* answer. God knows all of our needs, and He will provide!

The Dream Changer

Laura Broadwater

When I wandered into the living room, still rubbing the sleep from my eyes, I spotted my youngest son, Colton, huddled in a tiny ball on the couch.

Normally cartoons would have been blaring from the TV and he'd be happily munching away on a cup of dry Cheerios. But not *this* morning. Instead, he clutched his love blankie and stared into space.

The moment he spotted me, his bottom lip quivered and a flood of tears spilled down his cheeks.

"Oh, sweetie, what's the matter?" I rushed to his side, startled by such an unusual outburst from him.

"Mommy, I had another bad dream about Sarah!" Colton sobbed.

"What do you mean another bad dream?" I asked. This was the first time I'd heard him say anything about having bad dreams. "How many have you had?"

"Two. One last night and another one the night before."

"Do you want to tell me about your dreams?"

Colton sniffed and nodded his head. "In the first dream Sarah and her mom and dad were in town visiting. When they were on the highway, a rock flew through the window. It hit Sarah in her forehead and killed her."

"Oh, honey! Why didn't you tell me about this dream?" I asked, my mind reeling from the shock of his words. "You must have been really scared when you woke up."

"Uh-huh, but I was too scared to say anything," he said. "Then last night I dreamed Sarah's mom called and invited me to her funeral. And Mommy, I don't want to go to her funeral!"

He wailed, sending a new flood of tears down his cheeks.

I pulled Colton onto my lap and hugged him. My hands shook as I gently wiped at his tears. I couldn't wrap my head— let alone my heart—around what he'd just told me. I couldn't imagine how he must feel. My heart ached as I frantically tried to think of anything that might bring him comfort.

I knew he'd been missing his school friend Sarah since her family moved away, but obviously the loss was much greater than I had imagined.

"How about if I call Sarah's parents and see if you could talk to her?" I asked. "Would you like that?"

"Really?" Colton's eyes widened with excitement. "Could we?"

"Of course we can, but it's still pretty early in the morning, so we'll need to wait until later."

I felt his little body relax in my arms, so I decided to take a few moments and share a trick I often employed when I had a bad dream that wouldn't go away.

"You know, sweetie, sometimes even Mommy has bad dreams. You know what I do when I have them?"

"No, what?" he asked.

"I change the dream. For example, let's say I dreamed a white tiger was chasing me. When I lie back down and close my eyes again, I turn the white tiger into a fluffy white bunny rabbit."

Colton giggled. "That's silly, Mommy!"

"Well, of course it is, but it is better than dreaming about a white tiger chasing me."

After we'd talked for a while, the worry on Colton's face diminished. I even managed to coax him into eating some breakfast and watching his favorite cartoons.

By midmorning I decided it wouldn't be too early to make the call. Sarah's mom answered the phone and the two of us talked briefly. Without going into detail, I explained that Colton had had a bad dream about Sarah, and I felt it would really help if he could talk with her for a few minutes.

She thought the phone call would be good for Sarah, too. Apparently Sarah had been missing Colton—which really surprised both of us. It's not like the kids lived next door or knew each other for years. The only connection between Sarah and Colton had been through school—and they were only in first grade.

I handed the phone to Colton and watched his eyes light up. A smile quickly spread from ear to ear while he clutched the phone. I smiled as he paced back and forth, chattering like a little bird. When he laughed, his head bobbed up and down. It was as if his whole body had joined the conversation.

After I hung up the phone, I turned to Colton.

"Well, do you feel better now?" I asked, although I already knew the answer.

He nodded his head "yes," and I breathed a sigh of relief. I watched as he skipped out of the room in search of his brother.

"Hey, Justin, guess who I got to talk to on the phone?" he hollered.

The rest of the day passed without any mention of the bad dreams. When bedtime rolled around, I noticed that as Colton said his prayers, he added more emphasis on our usual prayer of asking Jesus to guard his heart and mind.

"Remember, sweetie," I said as I tucked his blankie under his arms, "if you have a bad dream, you can always change it."

Sunday morning I woke early, curious to see if the phone call with Sarah had ended the bad dreams. I peeked into Colton's room, not wanting to wake him if he were still asleep. Colton saw me and sat up.

"Guess what, Mom?" he said, smiling. "I had another dream about Sarah last night."

"You did?" I said, as I bit my lip. "Well, what happened?"

"I dreamed that I went to Sarah's funeral—"

"You what?!" I exclaimed. "Colton, why didn't you change the dream?"

"I didn't have to, Mom," he continued. "A man in white came and raised her from the dead."

"What did you say?"

"I went to the funeral and a man in white came and raised Sarah from the dead," he said in a matter-of-fact tone.

Suddenly I was reminded of Colton's bedtime prayer, of his asking Jesus to guard his heart and mind. The tears welled up in my eyes. Colton had chosen to trust Jesus with his dreams and with his friend's life. And Jesus had answered his prayer.

Colton's bad dreams about Sarah ended that night, but he still included her in his nightly prayers. The two stayed in touch with each other for years after their first phone call, writing letters to each other into their teenage years. For some unknown reason, they shared a bond that transcended the typical friendship.

I've often thought about Sarah over the last nineteen years, especially whenever someone mentions how God sends His angels to protect us from many dangers in life. I've heard people point out that we may never know what untold dangers we have been saved from until the glorious day when we stand before God in heaven. However, I have come to believe that sometimes we are blessed with a glimpse of His protection—even in a dream.

The Providential Dental Appointment

Delores E. Topliff

Shelly was a new student who came to our Christian school in British Columbia, Canada, in the fall of her junior year in high school. Her parents had divorced, her dad had remarried, and he and her stepmom were moving from the Pacific Northwest to Ohio, leaving teenage Shelly to board with a family connected to the school.

Since I was busy helping students enroll and get oriented, it took me a while to get to know Shelly. She was a bright, quiet girl with a round face and a blond Dutch bob with bangs. At times her emerald-green eyes twinkled, and her rare laughter was infectious. Her occasional one-line witticisms were zingers worth waiting for.

She didn't seem style savvy and gave the impression she didn't care, flaunting casualness as a badge of honor. Probably because of previous bad experiences, she seemed to reject others before they rejected her, as if acceptance didn't matter to her.

Except, of course, it did.

Shelly added brightly colored drawings to some assignments and to several envelopes she gave me.

Since my last name is Topliff, and I knitted winter hats for gift shops for extra cash, one envelope showed assorted fun styles of Topliff's Top Hats. But my favorite showed a wide-eyed blond girl hiding inside a treasure chest, lifting the lid, and climbing out. I didn't realize at first that the emerging girl was Shelly. I treasured those envelopes.

Her humor, shared with individuals, not the whole class, was hilarious, but few got the full picture of her many-faceted personality. Teaching her gave me more glimpses into the real person.

She was basically on her own that school year, and we noticed she didn't receive much mail, even though her parents were 2,500 miles away.

That winter my home was being remodeled, and while it was being worked on, my son and I stayed in the same home as Shelly did. The houseparents were kind, but hadn't yet connected closely with Shelly. I realized I actually had a ringside view of her life through reading her excellent writing and checking her schoolwork. I looked forward to what she would say, write, or do next, and she earned top grades. I understood her, and she knew it. At her age I had also lived away from home, so I knew from experience that a little love and understanding go a very long way.

One day Shelly got a surprising look at how much God loves her.

That glimpse started when my son went to the nearest town an hour away on the Alaska Highway and returned with two candy bars. I don't eat lots of candy, so I still had mine the next day.

During that lunch hour I had so much school prep to finish before afternoon classes that I rushed to our temporary home to complete it. Shelly hadn't felt well, was discouraged, and had skipped lunch, too. She heard me bustling around and knocked on my door.

She looked sad and alone, shifting from one foot to the other. "Will you please pray with me about something?"

"Of course, what is it?"

"My teeth are hurting, and I'm worried. I've been told my jaw is misaligned and I need it taken care of, or they'll have to break my jaw to fix it. It gives me tension headaches and I don't want worse problems. With Dad so far away, I don't know what to do. We don't have dental insurance or money for a visit. Please pray it quits hurting or that I get money for the dentist so I know I'm okay. This is really bothering me."

"I sure will." I patted her shoulder. "I understand why you're concerned."

It dawned on me that Shelly hadn't eaten, and I remembered my candy bar.

"Hey, I know you missed lunch. When my son went to town yesterday he brought back a candy bar. I'd like you to have it." I held out the treat.

"Really?" Her face brightened. "I love those. Thanks."

She walked toward her room, unwrapping the candy as she went.

Lord, do something special for that girl, I prayed.

Minutes later she knocked on my door again with a worried expression. She held her jaw with one hand, and a small object in the other. "I think I just broke a tooth. There was a rock in this candy bar."

"What? A rock?" I stared. "Oh no, that's terrible. How could that be?"

But when I looked at what she held in her hand, I thought she was right. It was a small, hard, red oval the size of my little fingernail.

"Where did you find this?"

"Inside the candy bar. When I bit down, my jaw popped. I think my tooth may have cracked."

"Wow! For sure you need a trip to the dentist. I'll contact the candy company and ask if they'll stand behind it."

Being an English teacher who believes in the power of communication, I wrote my best:

> Imagine my shock and disappointment when in my role as a high school teacher and assistant administrator, I gave a student one of your candy bars to encourage her, and she bit down on a rock inside, possibly cracking her tooth. I've enclosed the rock. I'm asking you to cover the cost of a basic dental exam, including X-rays, if necessary.

I signed off with a flourish and sent it off.

We soon received this reply. "We're sorry for your student's experience. We are analyzing the object and will report back to you."

A week later we received their official report:

> The offending item was not a rock. Lab analysis proved it to be a crystallized mass of super-heated sugar that dropped to

the floor of the mixing vat and hardened to the consistency of rock and ended up in the candy bar. Please do arrange for your student to have a full dental exam. Send us the dentist's findings and bill and we will cover payment.

Shelly made an appointment and saw the dentist. He found that although her jaw had popped, the structure of her teeth was fine. Her jaw misalignment was real but didn't need immediate attention, so she got by with X-rays and a basic cleaning. The candy company paid the bill, giving Shelly an immediately bigger and brighter smile. God showed His care for her worried heart by providing a dental appointment for her.

The whole event turned into a huge celebration for all of us. The candy company airfreighted two large gift boxes to our school filled with samples of every candy product they made. We rang the bell for school assembly. We had a great party, and I had a new convincing lesson on why it's important to learn excellent writing skills.

I was blessed to see Shelly flourish as she realized that God and others cared for her. And her success made me braver, so I could forget my own inhibitions to reach out to many others. Through several years, my extended family of former students now stretches into many nations.

Shelly begged to stay with us for her senior year and graduate, but her dad wanted her closer to their new home and the rest of their family. We stayed in touch, and I received more decorated envelopes.

When people say they doubt God has a sense of humor, I tell them Shelly's story and say that He has a keen one.

Shelly met and married Larry, a loving, warmhearted fellow with his own great sense of humor, and they have three great kids. Last Mother's Day, Shelly blessed me with a loving tribute on Facebook:

> I had a lot of troubles as a teenager, living far from family and no idea of what home was, although I longed for it. It hurts to remember that time. I felt isolated, misunderstood. I learned that when you don't appear to be happy, you might as well hang a sign around your neck that says, "Avoid Me." Most people felt I was unreachable. But at least one person figured out how to reach me, and she began to show me love. Her love and acceptance had a profound effect, and I believe it saved me.

Light of Peace and Deliverance

David R. Kenagy

The morning fog collected as dew and dripped from the mossy tree limbs that hugged our picnic table, tent, and car. In my five-year-old-boy enthusiasm, I jumped up and down.

Dad lit the burners on our green Coleman stove with a fiery whoosh. Mom cooked her tantalizing breakfast of bacon, eggs, and French toast. She served my dad, my two older brothers, and me on flimsy paper plates. To my delight, nothing slid off. This would be the first day of our best weekend camping trip to the Oregon coast ever, I thought.

"Now, don't forget to stay off that boat dock on the bay, Davey," Mom advised in her serious voice. "Until you learn to swim, it's no place for you to go alone. The water is sixty feet deep out there," she added, as if the depth would keep me landlocked. "We'll all walk over to the tide pools later, and you can catch minnows there."

"OK," I agreed, but with secret reservations.

On an earlier walk with Mom to the end of the now-prohibited dock, I had spied hundreds of tiny fish just under the water's surface. Anticipating a future fish-scooping expedition, I had begged Mom for something to use as a net. She offered her mother's bread pan, but it came with restrictions: "Don't use it without me there to watch you and certainly not on the dock. And remember, that pan was your granny's favorite and it's mine, too, so don't lose it."

"OK, Mom," I answered.

Later that morning, when we visited the tide pools, Granny's pan held starfish, sand crabs, and shells, but no fish. After eating a peanut butter sandwich for lunch, Dad went fishing up the river that entered the bay near our camp. Mom catnapped, my brothers played cops and robbers in the woods, and I kept thinking about minnows.

Because of my earlier walk to the dock with Mom, I knew the wide, sturdy structure was completely safe. I also concluded its thick wooden surface would make the perfect perch for kneeling and sweeping unsuspecting fish into Granny's pan.

I'd even noticed how the dock floated on two parallel lines of huge logs. Six-inch-thick moss covered the hefty timbers submerged below the dock's wood-planked walkway. This ideal minnow sanctuary hovered just within my arm's reach. With Granny's pan, I could flush the hiding fish into my metal net.

Dressed in a hand-me-down gray sweatshirt, jeans, and tennis shoes, I sat in camp ready for action. I planned a quick trip to the dock to dip out a few minnows. I could be back before anybody knew I'd left.

Easy, safe, and fun.

At just the right moment, I slipped away toward the nearby bay.

Just as I'd remembered, the dock's log floats housed billions of tiny fish. And they were all mine. The moss on the logs swayed in the current, exposing fish, then covering them. Irresistible.

I knelt on both knees, making a tripod with my knees and right forearm. Anchored this way to the dock, I was ready for a left-handed swipe at my prey. After pushing up my bulky sweatshirt sleeves, I dipped Granny's pan.

The fish above the submerged log swam faster than I expected. They all escaped. Inching closer to the dock's edge, I extended my reach toward the desired payload. Nothing.

Exasperated, I stretched down deep into the water and pulled hard with Granny's pan. My clever tripod collapsed and I tumbled over the side.

Water wrapped me in its smothering grip. But that didn't matter to me as much as my cloudy view of Granny's pan rocking side to side as it sank down and away from my desperate grasp.

Only after the pan vanished did I understand that I was also underwater. My sweatshirt bunched up around my shoulders, my jean legs waved in slow motion, and my shoes felt heavy with water.

I reached upward to grasp at the log supporting the dock above me. Its thick moss covering, my fishing ally, became my slippery enemy as my little hands slid off its slimy circumference. The more my arms and legs churned, the deeper I drifted under the water.

Looking up, I saw the mossy log and the distant sky above. The water's surface glimmered like the ice layer on a winter pond. Hard, impenetrable. And yet, during this hopeless struggle, a bright white circle of light caught my eye.

The light shone from above the water as if pointing at me below, and it completely absorbed my attention.

I stopped worrying about Granny's pan and felt no concern. As I sank powerlessly toward the bottom of the bay, I thought only of that radiant, happy light and felt embraced in peace.

I thought the bright light was the sun shining through the water. I have no memory of gripping the huge log float supporting the dock. I don't remember seizing the edge of the planks on the dock far above. I have no memory of pulling my drenched body back up onto the dock. I don't recall touching a muddy bottom or swimming to safety or anyone helping me.

I don't remember getting out of the water at all. But I do remember this: I had no fear. All was at peace. Even the chilled Pacific waters felt warm to me.

My next memory is of stumbling up the narrow trail from the bay to our campsite. Only this memory is not from my point of view on the trail. Instead, I've always seen myself on the trail as if I'm still back on the dock. I watch myself run up the trail toward Mom and Dad, repeating the only thing on my mind, "I lost Granny's pan! I lost Granny's pan!"

I entered our campsite still confessing my misdemeanor, oblivious to the message my soggy condition must have given Mom and Dad. Heavy wet sweatshirt, dripping jeans, and water squishing in my tennis shoes told the dreadful tale of a boy who'd fallen into the bay. After hearing my account of tumbling off the dock, Mom gathered me in her arms and asked, "How did you get out?"

"I don't know," I said.

Mom hugged me and held me close. I cried over Granny's lost pan. I saw Mom's tears but didn't understand them. Mom rocked me in her arms and helped me find dry clothes.

I've always questioned reports of angels when they follow the formula: "A bright light suddenly appeared." It's why I rarely tell my story.

But since that day I've learned something else about what happened to me. The Bible says, "The angel of the Lord encamps around those who fear him, and he delivers them" (Psalm 34:7).

From my earliest memories of praying with my granny, I knew God loved me and I loved Him. That granny, by the way, is the one whose pan I lost that day and whose prayers for her grandchildren never ceased.

But what, exactly, is this deliverance? Is it reserved for astonishing ocean rescues, or is it that and more?

The great peace, the comfort and quiet warmth of God's deliverance as I drifted under the water was my first taste of something I've known ever since that day, especially in times of crisis. It is the experience of the One who loves and abides inside me. His presence *is* His deliverance.

I've felt God's delivering presence encamped around me when wheeled into surgery as a teen, at my mother's deathbed, holding the lifeless body of my newborn grandson, and when the doctor told me I had a disabling nerve disease.

I've even known His deliverance on a regular day, when I pray and take my rest in Him. In those moments, just as on that day beneath the water, His righteousness, peace, and joy comfort me and bring great satisfaction and delight. My fears, anxiety, discouragement, and loss are buried in the depths of His love.

Angel on a Ladder

Karen Dorsey

"Pray for Rebecca."

Urgency overcame me, and I stopped to obey the Holy Spirit's prompting.

"Pray for Rebecca, now! She's in danger."

All of my focus turned to prayer for my sixth-grade daughter. After a few minutes, the urging left and I felt free to continue my tasks at hand.

My first speaking engagement at a women's retreat had provided the perfect opportunity for Rebecca to spend the weekend with her friend Bobbie. Rebecca loved to visit when Bobbie stayed at her dad's ranch two hours away from our home. Cell phones didn't exist then, so I couldn't quickly call to check up on her. As I struggled to keep my focus on the retreat and to trust that God had heard the prayer He prompted, God reassured me of Rebecca's safety. But I couldn't help but think of scenarios that might have happened.

Nestled between mountains with a river at the edge of the property, the ranch spoke of both serenity and adventure. Large pastures loomed as far as the eye could see. At the top of the property, a sturdy gate with the name of the ranch over it stood as a sentinel, keeping intruders out. Down the road a rustic two-bedroom farmhouse welcomed visitors. Two barns graced the property; the horse barn stood in front of the house, the larger cow barn down the road.

It was so serene at the ranch that if Bobbie and Rebecca had slept outside under the stars, the deer would have wakened them. But there was no lazy sleeping in at Bobbie's dad's house. I knew the girls got up early to help with chores.

I couldn't fathom any danger from the house. Surely the house couldn't have caught fire. Although Rebecca did often speak of the burnt grilled cheese sandwiches they ate for lunch or dinner.

"Mom, even you don't burn them as bad as Bobbie's dad."

There was a fireplace in the living room. In the cold, wet climate the girls spent hours in front of the fire, drying out after chores. Could it have started a house fire?

I didn't think so.

What about a four-wheeler accident?

Rebecca never complained about helping with chores at the ranch. She and Bobbie got to drive a four-wheeler around as they helped feed the animals and move hay. Bobbie's dad had even taught Rebecca to drive the vehicle.

One weekend the girls had tried to cross from the cow pasture to another pasture. Winter rains had turned the ground into a mud pit, and the four-wheeler had gotten stuck. Since Bobbie was driving, Rebecca got off to let her try to maneuver out of the mud with less weight on the vehicle. Bobbie ended up hitting the gas so hard that mud flew all over her.

Instead of offering to help push from behind, Rebecca had sat on the fence, nice and clean, far enough away from the action, and yet close enough to hear Bobbie yell in frustration.

"It's. Not. MUD!"

Yes, it was cow manure. Rebecca's laughter taunted Bobbie until Bobbie pulled her into the mess, too. They were both hosed off before being allowed into the house.

Could she have slipped in the river and hit her head on the rocks while fishing? Bobbie and her dad had taught Rebecca how to fish. The day she came home with a picture of the large fish she had caught, I heard more about how she gagged learning to gut the fish and clean it than how she caught it. Their house rule was "If you catch a fish, you eat it."

Though Rebecca hated fish, somehow she'd managed to eat hers.

The dangers of the ranch seemed as endless as the adventures. Had a cow or horse kicked her? What could have happened?

I continued to pray in between retreat sessions and through the night. I knew my husband could reach me on the camp manager's phone if necessary, but I didn't really expect a call. I expected to hear a story of a near miss.

But nothing prepared me for the real story Rebecca told when we both arrived home the next day.

That Saturday Bobbie's dad had needed to caulk some holes in the tin roof on the twenty-foot-tall horse barn. He invited both girls to climb the ladder and work beside him.

Heights didn't scare Bobbie or Rebecca, so they enjoyed helping. From the roof of the barn they could see all around the ranch. All went well until they finished.

"We were done, so we were climbing down," Rebecca explained. "Bobbie went first, I was second, and Bobbie's dad was still on the roof. The ladder leaned against a rafter that stuck out past the tin roof. And somehow the tin wasn't supported all the way to the edge because it gave way when I got close to the ladder. Bobbie screamed from the ground; her dad yelled from the roof."

Rebecca fell. Faster than she could think, her body and hands twisted and she caught the rafter that extended beyond the metal.

"Boy, Rebecca, the past couple of years of gymnastics saved you from a broken arm at the very least. Maybe even a broken neck."

"Yes. It was a long way to the ground, and I would have been badly hurt. But Mom, I was falling toward the ladder, on the other side of the rafter; my hands were turned the wrong way. There's no way I could have grabbed that beam." Her voice dropped to a whisper. "Mom, an angel caught my hands and flipped my whole body around. It wasn't me."

"Rebecca, what time did this happen?"

"Just after lunch."

Yes, the same time I'd felt the urgency to pray.

We both stood in awe of how God worked. I learned just how important it is to immediately obey a prompting from God, no matter how inconvenient or strange it may seem.

Rebecca learned that her God still works miraculously—and that guardian angels exist.

Seventeen years later she still says, "I literally have no idea how I caught hold of the rafter."

We both know God sent an angel to twist her around.

The Pink Vanity Miracle

Tom Cornelius,
as told to Joyce Williams

"I'm glad to see you, Tom," one of our volunteers told me as I walked into the door of the His Helping Hands ministry at our church. I'd just finished teaching a men's Bible study, but it was still early. As I shrugged off my coat, she continued, "A young couple is in the greeting area. They're looking for Christmas presents for their two daughters, two and six years old."

We weren't too far into the month of December, but already parents were coming to us, asking for help.

"Why don't you go rummage through the 'toy mountain' and see if you can find something for them?" she asked.

Our pastor at that time had a burden for the less fortunate. We have always had a heart for compassionate ministries at Central Christian Church in Wichita, Kansas, so before the new pastor had been there very long, our dream to reach out to the hurting of the community became a reality.

184

Even before we opened the doors of the building the Lord had miraculously given to us, a flood of items had been donated. We had hundreds of requests each week for clothing, furniture, food, and—especially in December—toys.

When I walked toward the enormous stack of toys, I thanked God once again for His incredible provision and the response of the warmhearted Kansans.

As I looked through the piles of toys, nothing seemed to touch my heart. Oh, there were lots of dolls, cute stuffed animals, and all kinds of playthings for little girls. But it was almost as though I could feel God leading me in a different direction.

I suddenly remembered the big plastic toys that were stuffed into a back room because they were so cumbersome. Moving aside a couple of plastic lawn mowers and a large rocking worm, I came across a little pink plastic vanity with a matching chair.

Somehow, I just knew that was the right thing.

I hurried back to the greeting area where the young couple was picking out some toys.

"Will a large toy be okay?" I asked the weary-looking mother.

She frowned. "Maybe we'd better take a look," she said. So she and her husband followed me into the back storage room.

When I showed them the pink vanity set, tears filled her eyes. "You must have read my mind!" she exclaimed.

Then she told me a story that brought tears to my eyes, as well.

"When my little girls saw our neighbors turn on their Christmas lights last night, they asked us if we were going to have Christmas this year," she explained. "My heart ached for our daughters. Because of several really tough situations, we had to tell them that getting gifts this year would take a miracle from God."

She pulled a tissue out of her pocket to wipe her tears. "At bedtime that night when our six-year-old said her prayers, she told Jesus that she knew He could do anything. Then she asked, 'Could you help us to celebrate your birthday this year?'

"As she was closing her prayer she added, 'Jesus, I love you, and I know you love my family. Please take care of my mommy and daddy, and let me have a pink vanity for your birthday.'

"I just knew there was no earthly way we could get that for her."

Then the mother said, "When I saw the pink vanity and chair, it was like a dream. It was just what our daughter had described when she asked Jesus to give her something special for Christmas!"

By that time all of us were grabbing tissues as we wiped our eyes. "God bumps" creeped down our arms as we realized God's special provision for this family.

As the young couple loaded the toys into their car, another volunteer asked them if their girls needed any clothes.

"Well, yes, they do. But we have everything we came to get and have been blessed so much. We don't want to take advantage."

The volunteer immediately took them back to the clothing section and let them pick out some items for their little girls. During that time they shared more of their story. The young father had cancer and was unable to work. The tired mother was trying to support the family with a minimum-wage job at a fast-food restaurant.

Our volunteers gathered that hurting father and mother into their arms and prayed for them. They shared words of encouragement and hugs. Then they helped load the car with the girls' Christmas gifts as well as household items and clothing for the entire family. They even found a Christmas tree and lights.

A warm glow wrapped around all of us as we watched the couple drive away. Their car had recently been involved in an accident, but now the misshapen vehicle was packed with all kinds of good things. The smiles on their faces were beautiful, and we saw a glimmer of hope in their eyes.

Truly we had witnessed a customized miracle from the Lord!

The faith of a little girl's prayer had been rewarded with God's answer to her specific request—a plastic pink vanity set!

I was reminded of the promise found in Matthew 7:7: "Ask and it will be given to you." Truly, the purest faith is a child-like faith.

Trapped Beneath
the Surf

Anne Garboczi Evans

Dad hit the brakes as the traffic inched to a crawl again. The refreshing scent of salty air blew through the windows.

"Are we there yet, Dad? Please, hurry up!" My brothers and I strained forward in our seat belts.

"A few more minutes," Mom said, passing back chocolate Tastykakes.

I leaned over to my three-year-old sister.

"You'll love the beach, Joy. The sand, the water, the waves."

A seagull cawed and dive-bombed the sand dunes ahead.

"I think I see the water." My little brother scooted to his knees.

There it was—a glimmer of blue on the horizon.

Dad slid into the beach parking lot, and we tumbled out of the car. We hoisted boogie boards over our shoulders and drink coolers under our arms. The beach umbrella and folding chairs almost got lost in the rush.

My flip-flops thumped across the sand. With a gleeful shriek, I ran into the water, deeper and deeper until a wave cast me to my knees.

We spent all morning in the waves, taking breaks to eat popcorn and lure vast packs of seagulls with Wonder bread.

As the sun reached its zenith and morning faded into afternoon, the waves became wilder. My dad took my little sister back to the hotel room for a nap. My mom rested under the umbrella. Since it was September, the beach was almost abandoned.

My older brother, fifteen-year-old daredevil that he was, went out farther and farther to catch the biggest waves. My little brother, ten-year-old Kyle, thought he could do everything my older brother could.

The ever-increasing waves splashed onto the pebbled beach, knocking down the towers I built. I held up my boogie board to block the surf. A wave plowed into me and pummeled me to my stomach.

I looked out to sea and another monstrous wave came crashing toward land. To the right, I saw my older brother riding high in the surf, both hands gripping his boogie board.

But I couldn't see Kyle.

Fifteen years later I was definitely experiencing one of those low weeks we all have at times in life. I was twenty-seven years old and the married mom of a two-year-old.

Six months earlier my husband had arrived home from a yearlong deployment. It had been a hard year. And now I was sick, the sickest I'd felt in a long time.

While I loved my son, the monotony of the stay-at-home-mom life, combined with my husband's long hours of working for the army, was wearing me down by inches. To top it off, one more childhood friend had just told me she no longer believed in God.

That made me think about the stories I'd been studying in Acts the past few months. I'd read that book at various times since my dad first introduced it to me twenty-five years earlier. But this time I saw something different. The chapters were full of wonders and miracles. Peter released from jail by an angel. Paul raising a dead man to life. The crippled beggar at the temple told to rise and walk.

If God is real, why don't we see this stuff today? I wondered. *Where are the angels? The deaf to hear, the lame to walk? The spiritual warfare?*

Is life merely the natural that we can see? That's what my atheist friend believed.

And that's what I was thinking about when my little brother, Kyle, now six-foot-three and a law school student, stopped by. We sat down for a late lunch as the Colorado sunshine blazed through my windows.

"Ever seen a miracle?" I asked, plunging my fork into the mashed potatoes.

My son, Joe-Joe, screamed that he didn't want the gravy *on* his potatoes.

"Oh, if your daddy was only home from work to deal with you," I wailed, in perhaps not my finest parenting moment.

"Actually, I think I might have," Kyle said.

My head swung over to my brother. "What?"

"Remember when we used to go to the beach as kids?"

I nodded.

"One time when I was about ten, I went out really deep by myself."

"Yes." I'd abandoned my fork to rest both elbows on the table.

"A wave crashed over me and I swallowed water. I struggled to get back up for air, but the surf held me down. I thought I was drowning."

Joe-Joe whined about the vegetables on his plate and begged for cookies. But for once, his wail didn't pierce right through my bones.

"Go on, Kyle," I said.

"I felt a hand wrap around mine and pull me to my feet. I gasped for breath and headed back to shore." Kyle speared the roast beef.

"And?"

"I thought it was Dad. But when I looked around, no one was anywhere near me." Kyle took a bite.

Chills ran up and down my spine. "So do you . . . I mean, was it . . . an angel?"

"I guess. I thought so at the time."

Goose bumps rose on my arms. My brother had felt an angel's hand fifteen years earlier. And I'd never even known it.

Maybe God was more active in this world than I'd thought, and I'd just never taken the time to look.

My dad has a PhD in physics, and he certainly taught me not to take every story as gospel truth. But evidence of the supernatural is so clear it can't be written off as mere coincidence.

Two thousand years have passed since Jesus walked the earth, raising the dead and causing the lame to walk. But that doesn't mean God is no longer supernaturally at work in the world. In a country like mine where the material world is king, people won't necessarily tell you about their experiences unless you ask.

So next time you're sharing a cup of coffee with a Christian friend and the conversation lags, ask him or her, "Have you ever experienced a miracle?"

You might be surprised at the response.

An Unexpected Answer

Ingrid Shelton

Even as a high school student, I wanted to be a nurse, and I was determined to make my wish come true.

So during my senior year, I sent my application for admission to the Regina General Hospital School of Nursing. Two weeks later I went to the doctor for my required physical examination.

Every day after that I waited eagerly for my acceptance, not realizing there might be a problem.

While I was contemplating life as a nurse on a Tuesday afternoon, the shrill ring of the hallway telephone interrupted my dream. When I rushed to answer it, the voice of the director of admissions at the school of nursing sent my heart into a spin.

"Miss Smith," he said, coming right to the point, "we cannot accept you into our nursing program. Your health is far too precarious."

I gasped for breath as his words slowly sank into my mind. I barely heard his explanation and only gave some rote response.

The unexpected results sent me reeling to my room. I knew I'd had some serious health problems in the past, including TB, but after a lengthy treatment I had been told I was well.

I had decided as a young teen to become a nurse primarily because I had spent time in various hospitals as a patient. I could identify with patients, especially children. I could feel their pain, their insecurity, and their loneliness.

The thought that I could not physically perform that role had never occurred to me. I'd always felt I could do anything I set my mind to. Even my high school teachers realized my poor health had not stopped me from achieving my goals.

They can't do this to me! my mind screamed as I flung myself onto my bed, tears blinding me. *How dare they stop me from becoming a nurse! Why do they get to decide what I should do with my life? What* will *I do?* I sobbed into my pillow.

Reaching for a tissue on the night table, I bumped into my little radio. On impulse, I turned the knob, hoping to drown the anguish in my soul. The harmonious sounds of an unfamiliar gospel song filled the room, and the chorus of male voices soothed my wounded spirit. Over and over I heard the words "God will take care of you." The rest of the words were lost to my distraught mind.

Suddenly an unusual thought came to me.

God! I should ask Him what He wants me to do.

God was a stranger to me during my childhood. Only in the last year had I realized that He existed and that He was Lord of the universe. Yet I was completely unaware that He was ready and willing to guide me in the way I should go. I didn't know all I had to do was ask Him about it and He would respond.

However, when I thought about asking the Lord, I didn't hesitate to drop to my knees. I thought this was the only correct position to address a holy God, because I recalled visiting a church once where people knelt to pray. I also noticed that these people prayed out loud.

I didn't know any prayers as such, but I knew how to ask. Not sure about the correct procedure to address God, I simply voiced my request without introduction: "God, what do you want me to be?"

As soon as I made my request, I heard an audible voice, sounding human, yet different: *"A teacher."*

Stunned, I turned my head, searching for the source of the voice.

But no one was there. I was alone.

That's when I realized that I had heard God's voice. He had answered, but it wasn't the answer I expected.

"No! No! Not a teacher! I'm not cut out to be a teacher!" I shouted my response.

Then I heard the voice a second time—lovingly, quietly, audibly: *"A teacher."*

Awestruck, I crawled back onto my bed.

"All right, God," I cried softly, a mixture of apprehension and relief. "I'll be a teacher."

As that new thought lodged in my heart, a deep peace settled in and a sense of excitement enveloped me. At the same time, I knew I would become a teacher not by choice, but by God's direction.

For many years I kept my experience of hearing God's voice a secret. No one would understand, I reasoned. I believed that people, including my family and friends, would think I had been dreaming or imagining a voice or would even think me mentally disturbed. How could I tell them I had heard God's voice—speaking to me?

I had never known anyone who had claimed to hear God's voice, and I was completely unaware that God had spoken to individuals in the Bible in surprising ways.

Even though I still felt inadequate and lacked confidence to prepare for such a noble profession, I enrolled in the teacher training college at the University of British Columbia.

I did not really look forward to teaching, and during the first year I often thought of changing my major. But the voice of God I had heard kept me going.

When I finally began to teach, I discovered that I really enjoyed teaching. My confidence grew by leaps and bounds, and I felt right at home in the classroom. I knew this was what I was meant to do in life.

After teaching for thirty-five years I retired, but I still tutor students God sends my way. I would rather teach than do anything else in life. I am grateful to God for not only guiding me unmistakably to a profession that was best for me, but also showing me that He answers prayer in a variety of ways.

Always.

A Still, Small Voice

Tim Hamblin

The porch had always been my happy place—until recently.
Now it just reminded me of my mom.

I climbed to the top railing of the porch, where I could see
the creek. It was full, the rains from the past few days causing
it to spill from its banks.

Mudholes covered the yard. If I hadn't been wearing my
Sunday best, it would have been fun to jump in a couple of
them, or maybe build a dam in one of the ditches that led to
the creek. I had already asked Papa if I could, but he reminded
me that my dad would come to get me soon, and I had to go
to a wedding with him.

I sat down on the bench in the corner of the porch, and Spot
came toward me and whined; he wanted to play in the mud, too.

"Sorry, boy, not today; maybe when I get back."

Papa had stopped swinging in the swing and wasn't singing
anymore. He was looking at me.

"Can I stay all night again, Papa?"

"Your dad will want you to go to church tomorrow, so probably not. Come here and swing with me."

I walked down the length of the porch, trying not to step on a nail. Then I hopped up on the swing next to Papa. He was short and thin, but strong as a bear. He had worked in the coal mines for more than twenty years, and it showed in his face, hands, and an occasional cough.

He put his arms around me, pulling me tight, my head resting on his chest. Then he started to swing . . . and hum. To me, those two sounds were the best sounds in the world.

"Mom wouldn't have made me go," I said.

"Probably not." The humming stopped and so did the swing. I looked at my papa. His eyes were sad now. One thing I had learned during the past couple of years was that adults lied, but they couldn't hide the truth from their eyes.

"I'm sorry," I said, patting him on the leg. I shouldn't have mentioned it. My mom was his daughter.

"So what do you want for your birthday?"

My seventh birthday was coming in a week.

"Mo . . ." I started and then stopped. "Nothing."

It had been a long couple of years. At first I didn't know that anything was wrong, and then Mom wasn't around for a couple of days. I kept asking Dad where she was, and he said she was visiting her sister. I asked him why I couldn't go, and he would always change the subject. I think I was four or so then.

She came back, but something was different. I didn't know what it was. She had always read a story to me when I went to bed, then sang to me softly until I fell asleep. The night she came back, she started the story and then began to cry.

"What's wrong?" I asked.

She shook her head and then told me that she needed to tell me something. It was the first time I had heard the word *cancer*, and I didn't know until then what a breast was. She talked about a big word that started with an *M*, which I still didn't completely understand, except I knew it was a very bad thing.

I went with her to Lexington for treatments. The doctors had cut the bad parts out but wanted to make sure they had removed everything. Her hair had fallen out, and she had been sick, sicker than I had ever seen anyone.

My aunt was with us and told me to be strong for my mom—so I helped as much as I could. Things got better then, and we went home.

Mom's red hair came back, and she claimed that she had more hair than ever. Again one night she told me she needed to tell me something. This time she told me that she was pregnant, and I was going to have either a brother or a sister in eight months.

The cancer came back during that time. She didn't tell me, but I knew. I could crawl into my closet and lean against the wall and listen to Mom and Dad talk.

It was back, but she wasn't going to do any treatments until after the baby was born. I got a brand-new sister, and then things really went downhill.

The last time I saw my mom, the ambulance came to get her. In our living room, the EMTs strapped her into a bed with wheels. She told my dad to get something from their bedroom and then told me to come close to her. I knelt on the floor next to the low gurney. She hugged me tight, kissing me on the forehead.

"I'm getting ready to go to heaven," she said, having trouble breathing, even with a mask over her face.

"I want to go, too."

"You have to take care of Dad and your sister," she said, smiling at me. "You have to be strong for both of them. When I'm gone, I will be in heaven, not under the ground. Remember, I will always love you, Timmy," she said, tears now streaming down both of her cheeks.

A few nights later, Dad came home and told my sister and me that Mom had gone to heaven. When I saw her in the box, her face had a huge smile. When she died, the first thing she must have seen was Jesus.

"Your dad's coming," Papa said, dragging me from my memories. I hadn't cried during the funeral or the days before. Any time I started to cry, I would remind myself to be strong.

I stood and walked toward the stone steps that led to the yard. Mamaw came out the screen door, motioning for me to give her a hug.

Dad pulled into the driveway, tooted the horn, and backed out into the road. He was in a hurry.

I jumped down the steps and walked down the stone path that led to the road. I hated new shoes. I turned, waved at Papa and Mamaw, and then continued along the path. I had made it halfway to the road when I heard a voice behind me.

"Don't go." It sounded just like Mom's voice. I stopped and turned around; no one was behind me.

The horn tooted and Dad rolled the window down.

"We're going to be late!" he yelled. I started back down the path.

"Don't go!" The voice was louder now and commanding. I turned around and ran back to the steps, taking them two at a time. I sprinted between Papa and Mamaw and through the screen door, through the living room, and into the back bedroom. I heard the car door slam. I knew Dad would be coming soon.

The door to the back bedroom had a lock. I opened the door, shut it, climbed on a stool, and turned the piece of wood that would keep the door from opening. I jumped down and crawled under the bed, scrambling as far away from the door as possible.

"Tim, let's go!" Dad yelled. The screen door slammed and he was at the bedroom door, banging on it. "I don't have time for this; I'm going to tan your hide."

I covered my ears with my hands and hummed to myself, shutting the noise out. I counted to a hundred and listened. He was still there.

I counted again and listened. I heard the car door slam. The engine revved.

I crawled from under the bed, my suit now covered with dust bunnies. I peeked out the window and watched the red Nova as my dad disappeared down the road and out of the holler.

"Timmy." It was Mamaw.

I unlocked the door and opened it. Waves of emotion hit me, and no matter how hard I tried, I couldn't stop them.

"I'm sorry," I said.

My grandma picked me up and carried me to her rocking chair. She hugged me close; she almost smelled like my mom. Soon I was asleep, and I had a dream. Mom was in heaven, and we were holding hands in a beautiful field. She explained to me that angels were watching over me and everything would be OK. We ran around the field for a long time.

The screen door closed and I woke up. I was lying in the bed in the room I had barricaded myself in. I could see Dad as he walked to the kitchen. I followed him; he had been crying. Mamaw and Papa were sitting at the table. He sat down and motioned for me to take a seat.

"Is Wanda OK?"

"She's fine. I was in a car accident driving back from the wedding. Rain started. I was a half mile from the house. I hit a slick spot in the road, and the car spun out of control. It spun so many times I lost count. It spun me over the curve; the car went down an embankment."

"Toward the river," Papa said.

"Yes, toward the river."

I knew the river was close to flooding in some areas of our town. The curve he was talking about was near the edge of the river even when it hadn't rained for a while.

"A small tree stopped me about five feet from the river. Timmy, if you had been in the car, we would have broken the tree and gone into the water."

He was crying now. I was crying, too. I gave him a big bear hug.

"Thank you, Jesus. . . and Mom," I whispered.

Assurance in Prayer

Patricia L. Stebelton

The weather was mild—too mild for December in Michigan. The temperature felt more like late October, and yet overhead clouds warned that storms were headed our way. The stirring inside my chest told me a storm was building in there, too, and I was powerless to stop it.

I stared moodily through the screen door to the concrete porch where my father worked intently on his project. He wore a grim expression and a determined look as he tried to organize two inextricably tangled strings of large outdoor Christmas lights.

How long will Dad stay this time? I wondered. His unpredictable comings and goings the last couple of years had left our family in emotional turmoil and jeopardized his relationship with Mom. The safe feeling I'd once had within our family had dissolved amid constant upheaval and conflict.

As I watched Dad work with the outdoor lights, I realized I had warring emotions regarding my somewhat estranged father. Even laying aside my protective feelings toward my mom, I still had to deal with a long string of broken promises.

What had happened to the hero of my childhood memories?

My memory bank held a scrapbook with unexpected snapshots of happier times that would suddenly appear. I saw us camping on the steep banks of the Au Sable River, where, as a four-year-old, I posed with the gigantic fish I'd caught—with help, of course. I held the fish high so Daddy could see my smile when my mother took the picture. Our big, roomy tent was pitched behind me, where I would snuggle down and listen to outdoor sounds in the darkness, my eyes still bright from the day's excitement, my nostrils tingling with the scent of fresh pine.

My brother David came along too late to know the happier times; he'd never ridden on Daddy's lap out on a country road, with the sun flooding the front seat of our 1946 Ford, or taken trips to family reunions in Ohio. Was I angry about that, too, or just sad—or maybe both?

At twelve, I felt I was now more an adult than a child, and I was able to look at the circumstances more objectively than my brother might.

Unfortunately, the heavy sigh that slipped from my mouth belied those thoughts. A deep aching inside me wanted desperately to trust what I was seeing now—my father engaging in our family Christmas activities. I wanted to hold on to the dream that my family would be united this Christmas—the way it used to be before that tragic, bleak day so many years ago when my baby brother died suddenly three days before Christmas. Was that when Dad first began to act differently, long before David was born?

I'd experienced so many disappointments that I was almost afraid to trust my father again, worried that the hope inside would turn sour. I'd prayed that God would fix my broken family for what seemed an eternity, but I was now afraid to believe it might actually happen. Could my fragile faith handle another disappointment?

Dad put the small stepladder on top of the porch near the edge where it curved to drop down to the first step. With his hands on his hips, he gazed upward, seemingly to study where the roofline and soffits met.

Pressing my face against the screen, I called, "Dad, do you want me to help you? I could hold the ladder."

I felt suddenly like I wanted to be a part of what was happening.

"No thanks. Sometimes more people on the job only get in each other's way. I've got this covered. The lights will be up in no time," he replied.

I watched him climb the stepladder, holding the first string of untangled lights. He reached down to the holding tray to grab the hammer and the first of a series of hooks.

Marking his place on the roofline, Dad stretched his body upward from the top ladder step and arched slightly to the left to position the first hook above the entrance to the porch.

As he aimed his hammer to strike, Dad's arm pulled back slightly and his body swayed to the left. The ladder wobbled and he was thrown down to the concrete walk below, his right hand still clutching the string of lights.

Blood gushed from his hand. In shocked panic, I clung to the screen door and yelled, "Mom! Come quick! Dad fell. He's hurt!"

My heart screamed for God to do something—to fix my dad.

I had no idea what to do. I couldn't even move.

My first thought was *Will he die?*

Sucking in a fortifying breath, I ran outside and down the steps.

When I saw the blood up close, my stomach lurched and my head felt woozy. Dad's palm was cut in several places, jagged pieces of broken bulbs protruding from the wounds.

My mother raced out the door and down the steps. She knelt and gently wrapped his hand in a cloth. Taking one quick look at me, she told me to go back inside the house and wait.

Her jaw set, Mom tore up the stairs again and into the house to call for help. Wishing I could do something, I sat on the sofa facing the door so I could see outside.

Then and there, I began to have a serious heart-to-heart talk with the Lord. Not quite a year had passed since I'd asked Jesus to be my Savior. I strongly believed that Jesus was God's Son and that He loved me and had died for me. Since that day, I'd felt an indescribable sense of acceptance and never forgot that special moment when I knew I belonged to Him.

I thought of Jesus as my best friend. Maybe that's why I had such an overwhelming sense of comfort and assurance.

The worry was gone, leaving peace in its place. As I watched my mother rush by with her first-aid kit, I remembered that Dad had taken a first-aid course. Mom had said she'd learned just enough to scare her that she might not do the right thing. I hoped she was doing the right thing now.

When help finally arrived to transport Dad to the hospital, Mom came back inside to sit with me. She inhaled deeply and wiped her face, looking worried. Noticing my calm state, her countenance sobered even more.

"I wonder if you understand how badly your father is hurt," she said. "The gashes in his hand are quite deep. Of course there's no way of telling how much damage has been done, but I'm concerned that he might lose the use of his hand."

Mom paused, her lips pressed tight. "There's no doubt they'll keep him overnight, but I'm sure someone will call when they know more. I think he will have a long recovery and will need our help when he comes home."

She sat slumped on the edge of the sofa as if the weight of the world were on her shoulders.

Without wavering, I smiled at my mother. When I spoke, my tone was matter-of-fact.

"Don't worry. It's going to be okay, Mom. I do realize Dad is hurt badly, but he's going to be all right. I know he is. I prayed."

I had the assurance in my heart that Dad would recover. It couldn't have been plainer to me if God had spoken audibly or written it across the sky in blazing color.

My mother eyed me curiously. Forcing a weary smile, she nodded and stood. She walked back into the kitchen without another word.

It was a few days before Dad returned home, his hand heavily bandaged. As Mom predicted, he did need our help. Months of therapy and rehabilitation followed before he could move his fingers, but eventually he recovered full use of his hand. I now knew that whether or not our family ever returned to the way it had been when I was younger, or the way I'd hoped it might be, we would be all right. I had the assurance written on my heart that God was capable of caring for those who put their trust in Him.

A few years later, my mother trusted Jesus as her Savior, and we had the joy of praying together about many things. When she died unexpectedly, I realized that I had never explained to her what took place in my heart the day Dad fell and injured his hand. But knowing she is happy with Jesus, it's possible that she already knows. If not, I'll look forward to sharing it with her someday when we are together again.

Jesus in My Pocket?

Kathy Sheldon Davis

Joanne's teacher tapped the chalk on the blackboard as she wrote the day's assignment, leaning to the left with each careful stroke. Since the chalk trail started near the top of the board, Joanne was sure she'd have enough time for a quick adventure with the tiny doll she had hidden in her desk.

"Joanne."

How could her teacher know what she was doing? She tightened her grip on Dolly. Lifting her eyes but not her head, she answered, "Yes?"

"Would you bring your desert art project to the front of the classroom to share with us, please?"

"OK." Joanne lifted the drawing from the desk and apologized quietly to Dolly, looking around to see if her classmates had noticed.

After morning recess, Joanne sat quietly before her math problems, tapping her pencil on her nose. The pencil slipped from her fingers and rolled off her desk. When she bent over to retrieve it, she spied on Pete, who was busily working his equations. Joanne hated math, and third-grade math was the worst. She didn't like her annoying seatmate, Pete Findley, either. All boys were weird, but Pete was weird *and* mean.

Having a girl sit next to her would have been a lot more fun for Joanne, but Mrs. Addington thought Pete would settle down if he sat next to her. Sometimes it wasn't fun being a good girl.

At the end of the school day, the cluster of girls in the back of the room giggled and squealed. The boys pushed and punched. Someone said they should have a birthday party every day so they could have cupcakes every day. Joanne pinched a cupcake crumb in her fingers for Dolly to enjoy later.

She turned her head to see if Dolly was still safely hidden. She thought about how she loved having her little friend nearby.

Dolly would never stop being her friend. Dolly was never grumpy or mean. Joanne scrunched her shoulders at the thought of her little sister, Sandy, hugging Joanne's old doll, the one she'd traded for Dolly.

Since she was the oldest, Joanne felt she deserved to have the four-inch cheerleader doll. It had been easy to convince Sandy to trade her birthday present for the larger doll that had two outfits, two diapers, and a baby bottle.

Dolly was perfect for hiding in Joanne's coat pocket on the way to school every day, perfect for being the friend she'd always wanted.

Two days later, the project in Sunday school was to color a big red Valentine heart with a cross inside it and to memorize Matthew 28:20. The heart represented Joanne's life, and the cross represented Jesus in her life.

After practicing the Scripture verse, "I am with you always, to the end of the age" (Matthew 28:20 ESV), the class had their snack of crackers and Kool-Aid.

The Sunday school teacher, Miss Beymer, sat on the small chair across the table from the children and asked, "What do you think about Jesus always being with you?"

Freddy squirmed. "It's creepy, if He comes in the bathroom with me."

Laughter filled the room.

Miss B smiled. "It doesn't bother Jesus, Freddy. He made you."

When the room quieted, Joanne asked, "Does Jesus really see everything?"

"Yes, He does." Miss B laid her hand on Joanne's shoulder. "He said He is always with us, and He never breaks His promises."

She pointed to the Valentine Joanne was coloring. "He's right there in your heart."

The next day was dance day at school, and Joanne loved dancing. The music made her feet happy, and the movements made her heart happy. She didn't even mind holding a boy's hand (unless it was Pete's). He laughed when he squeezed the girls' hands too hard and made them pull back in pain, and he had a wart on his finger. Maybe she'd only pretend to touch his hand.

When the line at the drinking fountain shrank and the children rushed to their seats, Pete's math paper floated to the floor. He sat down to pick it up, but it was pinned under his chair. When it ripped in two, he groaned and kicked the desk.

The teacher reminded the students to speak quietly with their neighbors.

Our neighbors? Several Sundays earlier, Miss Beymer had moved the figure of a bearded man in a robe across the flannelgraph board. She called him a neighbor. He didn't look like Pete.

But as Joanne glanced at Pete next to her, she realized he was her neighbor whether she liked him or not.

"Love your neighbor as yourself" (Mark 12:31).

That was a memory verse from a long time ago, but it came into her mind from nowhere. She put her hand to her chest—sure that Jesus was speaking to her in her heart.

Joanne pictured in her mind a cartoon on TV of a girl falling in love. Her hands were clasped and stars were twirling in her eyes. Flower petals floated above her head, and birds chirped. Love was heavenly, but she didn't like Pete Findley.

People didn't like the man in the Sunday school story, either, but the lesson said Jesus wanted us to be kind to everyone.

"Love him as yourself. Love him like I love you."

Joanne clamped her mouth shut and stuck out her chin. *Dying on the cross didn't feel good to Jesus,* she thought, *but He did it to obey His Father in heaven—because He loved us.*

Jesus didn't say I have to marry Pete. He just wants me to treat him like I would want to be treated if I ripped my paper.

Her teacher had said the world could spin in only one direction and couldn't change course, but as Joanne's eyes wandered to the globe on the file cabinet, she felt something in her world shifting.

She reached into the back of her desk. "Would you like some tape to fix your paper?"

Pete looked at her like she'd grown antennae on top of her head.

"Sure. OK."

She held out her prized roll of tape, knowing he might spoil it or refuse to return it. But that didn't matter. Even if Pete would never be nice to her, she would be nice to him because Jesus told her to.

During the circle dance that afternoon, when the boys changed partners and spun them around, Joanne saw Pete coming up next. She heard Jesus in her heart say, "There's your neighbor." This time she wouldn't look for a way to avoid touching him. She clamped her teeth, smiled, grabbed his hand, and curtsied. She found it was actually fun to dance with joy instead of worrying about warts.

Pete seemed to enjoy it, too, because he skipped more exuberantly than necessary when they parted. And he hadn't hurt her hand.

On Friday morning, Joanne slipped Dolly from her coat pocket to her hiding place, only to turn around and catch Pete watching her, his eyebrows lifted above his conspiratorial grin. Her breakfast felt heavy in her stomach as she pushed Dolly deep into the darkness of her cubby and walked to the cloakroom to hang up her coat.

He knew.

Her chest expanded as dread filled her mind. She was going to lose Dolly. Pete would steal the doll or tell on her. She'd be sent home from school with a note to her parents.

With her shoulders slumped, she returned to her desk.

Jesus told her, *"Remember, I am with you always."*

She exhaled and trusted His words. Jesus promised to always be with her. Maybe He would help her keep Dolly.

Turning her head toward Pete as she took out her social studies book, she saw his smirk.

"I'm gonna tell," he whispered.

Joanne knew she was doomed to a life of loneliness. What would she do without her little friend?

The bell rang at 2:30, and her teacher dismissed the class. Joanne kept her head down as she lifted her coat above her shoulders and slipped her arms through the sleeves. She knew Dolly had to go home and never come to school again.

Waiting until most of the kids were gone, she slid Dolly from her desk and into her homework folder and left the room.

When she'd passed the principal's office, she stuck her homework into her library book and dropped Dolly into her coat pocket.

Outside, she looked up and down the street for a friend to walk home with, but everyone was gone. Then a glint of blond hair caught her eye in the gutter.

"Dolly, how did you get there?" Joanne picked up the doll and brushed the dirt from her ponytail.

Reaching into her pocket to look for a hole, she discovered a rumpled Sunday school drawing of a Valentine and a cross. She was puzzled because usually she gave her drawings to her mother after church. Then she read the verse.

She stopped breathing. It was the wrong verse! She was certain the verse had been "I am with you always." But it said, "You are my friends if you do what I command. . . . This is my command: Love each other" (John 15:14, 17).

Joanne turned the page over and found her name in her handwriting on the back. She looked at the coloring again. Sure enough, the Valentine was pink instead of red. When had she colored this one?

Her cousin's face came to mind. Oh yes! They'd spent Valentine's Day at her uncle's church in Newburg. That's why this drawing hadn't made it into her mother's hands.

Now, when she felt friendless and alone, she'd found the verse that reminded her that Jesus was her friend. Had He gone into her pocket and pushed Dolly out, just to get Joanne's attention?

Joanne laughed and shoved Dolly deeper into her pocket. She hugged her library book and homework and skipped the rest of the way home, doing a little dance step at the corner. Wherever Jesus was, whether in her pocket or in her heart, He was her friend and He'd never leave her. The world was spinning in the right direction after all.

In My Distress, He Heard Me

Audrey Carli

My friends Marla, Ellen, Dotty, Jane, and I were talking a mile a minute after school while walking to our local hangout to chat and sip sodas. Suddenly an engine hummed as a car pulled to the curb beside us.

"Audrey, your dad just had emergency surgery! I'll take you to the hospital to see him right away." It was my Aunt Miriam.

My friends' smiles faded. "Bye, Audrey." Their caring voices blended with their hopeful messages for my father's recovery.

"Thanks so much!" I called, waving as we drove away.

On the drive to the hospital, my aunt filled me in on my dad's situation.

"Your Uncle Larry said your father was lifting the end of a heavy log, when he doubled over in pain. He helped your father to the truck and drove him to the hospital. The surgeon had to mend a ruptured ulcer, serious because the tear had caused the contents of his stomach to spill into the abdominal cavity."

I was shocked at her words. I knew Dad's situation could be fatal.

"As you know, this is a small hospital," my aunt said, "but they will do all they can to stabilize your father's condition before he is transported to a larger facility."

Mom, Uncle Larry, and Aunt Miriam had waited until the surgery was completed midafternoon. Then Aunt Miriam had been sent to locate my siblings and me and had found me first.

As my aunt and I hurried along the hospital corridor, she whispered, "That tall man ahead of us is the new Dr. Jason from a big university hospital downstate. He just left your dad's room. I hear the hospital staff is very glad to have him."

"I wish Dad were in that big city hospital with all the latest equipment."

Aunt Miriam nodded. "Your father is very weak now. He'll need critical care for a while before he can be moved."

It was hard not to cry as I realized my dad could die.

When we entered Dad's room, I rushed into Mom's arms. We hugged for a long time, as if clinging to hope.

"We'll just keep praying," Mom whispered.

Dad's eyes were closed and his legs moved in spasms under the white blanket. A nurse told us the spasms were normal and would subside.

She patted my arm and whispered that everything was being done that could be done.

My hope rose with continued prayer that Dad would survive. We loved him and needed him. He didn't appear young from my teenage perspective, but he was not yet forty.

Mom stood beside the bed, gazing at Dad, as if to memorize his features.

"Lord, please save my father's life. We need him!" I whispered.

As a nurse spoke to Mom, I concentrated on the hope that Dad would open his eyes and speak to me his usual "Hi! How was your day at school?"

But his eyes remained closed, and he seemed so still.

My heart pounded as I continued to pray, *"Dear Jesus, please save my father's life. Thank you, Jesus."*

Before long, Aunt Miriam was dropping me off at home, where my sisters Ann and Jean and brother, Allen, wondered where everyone had been. They gasped at hearing the news of Dad's emergency surgery. Then they were rushing off in Aunt Miriam's car for their turn at the hospital.

I was shivering with stress after they left. I wished they were going for a pleasant drive instead of to the redbrick hospital on Ross Street.

The silence in our home was like an invisible blanket smothering my peace. Torn with anxiety, I grabbed the worn Bible from the shelf, knelt by the sofa, and prayed. "Dear Jesus, please help Dad get well again. I am so eager to know how he is. Please lead me to a Scripture verse that will ease my worry. Please help Dr. Jason to help Dad. I am so thankful for his university hospital training. I pray in Jesus' name. Amen."

I opened the Bible and my gaze fell on the first words on the page.

Hope sang in me as I read Psalm 120:1, "In my distress I cried to the Lord, and He heard me" (NKJV).

"He heard me!" I exclaimed.

I prayed my thanks until I fell asleep on the sofa.

The next day, we learned that our small hospital's equipment was indeed insufficient for Dad's needs. However, Dr. Jason had devised a pump to remove the foreign contents of Dad's abdomen. Two jugs with connecting tubes attached at different levels to his body gradually collected the fluid. Dr. Jason's training had enabled him to create the pump procedure. And it led to my father's eventual recovery.

Yes, the Lord hears us as we cry out to Him in prayer, whether in silent petition or spoken aloud.

Dad came home from the hospital, and he returned to work.

And our family was reunited. Thanks be to our Lord Jesus Christ!

The Night of the Jackal

Sylvia Stewart

The jackal's howl that grim night made my situation seem much worse than it was.

My missionary parents, my brother, Jim, and I had first arrived in Africa a few days short of my sixth birthday. Palm trees lining the dirt airstrip seemed to fly by as our plane taxied to the terminal, a small thatched-roof building standing in the shade of the palms. The next day my family and I started our long journey from Leopoldville (now Kinshasa) into the bush country to our mission station in the Ituri region of the eastern Belgian Congo, now called the Democratic Republic of the Congo.

Our new life held many joys. Traveling to our new home, my brother, Jim, and I were excited to see a variety of animals, including baboons and long-haired, black-and-white colobus monkeys bounding among the trees. Antelopes and zebras fed on the tropical vegetation. When we came to a clearing in the great rain forest, we saw elephants, Cape buffalo, gazelles, and wild pigs. Our parents told us that leopards, hyenas, and jackals also prowled in the night.

As we adjusted to living in Africa, we learned to enjoy eating buffalo or gazelle for dinner. With our Congolese friends, we ate roasted field corn on the cob, fried ants, roasted or boiled manioc root, and "bogos" (cooked green plantain bananas). At home, we could eat all the bananas, pineapple, and mangoes we wanted, and we learned nothing was sweeter than freshly squeezed juice from tree-ripened oranges. What an exciting new life!

My parents homeschooled us until I finished the second grade. During our recesses, Jim and I fed our pet monkey or played house under the shade of an oleander bush, watching carefully for snakes or spiders that might drop into our play area.

Eventually, Mama and Daddy decided Jim and I needed to go to Rift Valley Academy, a Christian boarding school in the highlands. Not only was the air cooler, but we could also enjoy fresh milk, because tsetse flies didn't live in the highlands to kill off the cattle. We would also be away from malaria-bearing mosquitoes.

Our new school had no telephone, so we couldn't talk with our parents for the three months of our school term. If we needed Mama or Daddy, our dorm parents would have to send a message by radiophone. Because of rough roads, if our parents came to visit, it would take ten hours to drive to our school, even though they were only 350 miles away. So we kept in contact through weekly letters.

Living in a dorm with lots of other girls was fun for a while. However, a few weeks into my boarding-school experience, I lost the fascination of being "a big girl on my own." Reality had set in.

I quickly learned that a smart missionary kid chose the top bunk because none of her friends could sit on it and mess up the covers. I felt disturbed when some girls borrowed things without asking for permission.

I missed our pets; they were not allowed at boarding school. However, we climbed trees, played Pilgrims and Indians, making "wampum" from chains of nasturtium stems to redeem the captured—and had a picnic in the pine forest at midterm.

Although Jim attended the same school, he stayed in the boys' wing of the dorm. He played with the bigger boys on the playground, and I had no interest in their rougher games. My class met in a different room from Jim's, so I usually saw him only from a distance. And finding him at mealtimes among the seventy-five kids swarming the dining room didn't seem to work.

The worst part of my day was bedtime. Loneliness would smother my heart like the stuffy mosquito nets draped from the ceiling over my bed at home.

Then came the night I heard the jackal howl. I turned over every few minutes trying to find a comfortable position. The tropical moonlight beaming through the window made a white rectangle on the floor, causing me to be even more wakeful and restless. I watched the rectangle creep toward the door as the minutes passed.

Memories of home and longing for my parents flooded my mind, and intense sadness clutched my heart. I rolled over onto my back, and tears sprang into my eyes. The white window curtains swished back and forth over the windowsill on puffs of warm breeze.

I'm alone—so far from my parents. The jackal howled again at the moon. Even though I knew a jackal was just a wild dog, his mournful call made me feel sadder. *I won't be able to see Mama and Daddy for a long time. I can't even phone them.*

And what if I get sick or hurt—who will take care of me? I'm all alone, and I'm only a kid. I guess I'll have to take care of myself, but I don't know how to do that.

I started to cry.

Maybe Mama and Daddy don't really want me anymore. I suppose teaching us kids at home was too much trouble.

The jackal howled again. The long yap and wail of a wild dog's despair echoed my own. Tears trickled through the hair at my temples and down into my ears. I pulled my pillow out from under my head and clamped it to my face, trying to smother the deep sobs that erupted. Every boarding-school kid knew it was "sissy" to cry.

I guess my parents don't want me. Maybe God doesn't even want me! I'm alone. All alone!

I felt like my heart would break.

Then, in the suffocating darkness under my stuffy pillow, God spoke to my heart as clearly as if He had been standing right beside my bunk.

"Of course your mama and daddy love you! And you're not alone. Don't be afraid. I am with you. Go to sleep now."

Even though the comfort seemed small at the time, my sobbing eased and the knot in my chest relaxed. Sniffing back the tears, I turned on my side, jammed the pillow back under my head, and fell asleep.

After that experience, I've never again doubted God's presence with me or whether He or my parents love me. When I feel alone, abandoned, or discarded, I remind myself that God will never leave me. "God has said, 'Never will I leave you; never will I forsake you'" (Hebrews 13:5).

The jackal's howl of despair may echo in our soul at times, but no matter where we are or in what situation we find ourselves, God is always near to protect and comfort us. We are never alone.

About the Contributors

Dawn Aldrich is an award-winning children's author, children's television co-host, and blogger. Dawn blogs at Dawn's New Day, Encouragement Café, {re}fresh, and Christian Children's Authors.

Valerie Avery is director of Embraced by Hope, a ministry to the wounded individually through her private practice and corporately in group therapy, retreats, and seminars. She is a trainer with Open Hearts Ministry and an international writer and speaker.

Kate Barrows (not her real name) is a barista in Hermosa Beach, California. Among other things, she likes music, art, fitness, biking, Harry Potter, and eating organic food.

James Stuart Bell owns Whitestone Communications, a literary development agency, and is the compiler of this volume and over thirty-five more of its kind.

Laura L. Bradford is an award-winning poet and author. Her works have appeared in numerous CHICKEN SOUP FOR THE SOUL and Guideposts books, as well as in Gary Chapman's *Love Is a Verb*.

Catherine Ulrich Brakefield is the author of four books and numerous short stories. Her most recent is *Wilted Dandelions*. Find her at www.CatherineUlrichBrakefield.com or www.facebook.com/CatherineUlrichBrakefield.

Laura Broadwater is a contributing author in *A Cup of Comfort Devotional for Mothers* and *The Mommy Diaries*.

Wanda J. Burnside is a poet, author, playwright, and publisher. She is founder of Write the Vision Ministries, Media Productions, and *The Lamp Newsletter*.

Audrey Carli is from Iron River, Michigan, and writes for Christian publications, including *Guideposts*. Her three books include *Jimmy's Happy Day, When Jesus Holds Our Hand,* and *Valiant Victory*.

Joann Claypoole is the author of DOVE STORIES, a children's chapter book series. She is a wife, mom, and salon/spa owner in sunny Central Florida. She features in Yvonne Lehman's MOMENTS book series.

Tom Cornelius is a tireless volunteer at his church in Wichita, Kansas.

Julie B. Cosgrove writes for several publications and Christian women's websites, as well as her own blog, *Where Did You Find*

God Today? She has also authored a number of books. Find them at www.juliebcosgrove.com.

Tracey Dale-Akamine resides in King of Prussia, Pennsylvania, with her husband, Brian, and two daughters, Hannah and Emiko. Tracey and her husband are church planters.

Kathy Sheldon Davis, a media assistant, proofreader, and copy editor, lives in Oregon with her husband, Jerry. She posts devotionals and parenting tips on her blog and also writes historical fiction.

Lisa Plowman Dolensky is mom to three miracles and celebrates twenty-eight years with her husband, Ed. She is a faculty member of The Capitol School in Tuscaloosa, Alabama.

Karen Dorsey has been an elementary schoolteacher for thirty-one years. She is married and has two daughters and two grandsons.

Anne Garboczi Evans is a counselor. She's currently writing a book about world religions entitled *No Fear: My Tale of Hijabs, Witchcraft Circles, & the Cross.* Get her e-newsletter at annegarboczievans.blogspot.com.

Dianne Fraser lives in Busselton, Western Australia, and works as a media liaison for Cornerstone Christian College. She is married to Neil and they have two miracle children, Jayden and Callum.

Bev Gattis worked at Teen Challenge in New York and taught typing, art, journalism, and Bible at a Christian high school. She is an author of two books under the pen name Bella Gregor.

Verda J. Glick, missionary in El Salvador, tells about her husband's kidnapping in her book *Deliver the Ransom Alone.* Her writing has appeared in more than fifty publications, including *Guideposts.*

Lynnette Goldy lives in Colorado, where the plains meet the mountains. She is an Orthodox Christian joyfully seeking to grow into God's likeness.

Anna M. Gregory lives with her husband, Dennis, and has five sons, seventeen grandchildren, and one great-grandchild. Her published devotions have appeared in *The Secret Place, The Upper Room,* and others.

Tim Hamblin is the author of THE 12 GUARDIANS, a Christian thriller series. He lives in Hazard, Kentucky, with his wife and daughter.

Judith Victoria Hensley is a retired middle-school teacher, weekly newspaper columnist, photographer, blogger, and speaker. She has authored books on Appalachian folklore, middle-school chapter books, and Christian fiction.

Sandra L. Hickman is an evangelist and Christian writer from Western Australia. She writes nonfiction stories, poetry, and songs. Sandra's first book, *The Letter,* was published in 2015.

Suzelle Johnston lives in the Black Hills part of the year and the foothills of the Catalina Mountains the rest of the year. All the time she lives with a husband she pesters incessantly and two dogs that pester her.

David R. Kenagy, a native Oregonian, serves as an ordained elder of the Evangelical Church of North America and is a dean emeritus of the Willamette University College of Law in Salem, Oregon.

Debra McCann resides in Delaware with her husband and daughter. They attend church in Bear, Delaware, where she serves on the café ministry team. She writes devotionals and magazine articles.

Diane M. Nunley is a retired nurse and lives in the Cumberland Mountains of West Virginia. She has been published in professional journals and devotional books.

Linda O'Connell is a teacher, published writer, and great-grandma. She and her husband live in the Midwest, but prefer the beach. Find her at http://lindaoconnell.blogspot.com.

Kendy Pearson and her husband, Kevin, live in Oregon with seven chickens, a cat, and a precocious dachshund named Addie.

Jeanne M. Phelan has been married for forty years and has four children and five grandchildren. A licensed foster parent, she has been published in *The Upper Room, The Lookout,* and others.

Trish Propson owns Cornerstone Communications Company and directs rekenekt, offering hope and restoration to families. Learn more about Trish and rekenekt at www.cornerstone-comm.org.

Elissa M. Schauer has written children's spiritual development curriculum for the past decade. She lives near Chicago with her husband and three children.

Ingrid Shelton is a freelance writer and a retired teacher. She is an organic gardener who grows her own vegetables and fruit. In her spare time she visits shut-ins.

Heather Spiva is a writer from Sacramento, California. She loves reading, spending time with her boys, and selling vintage clothing from her online store. Find her blog at www.heather-spiva.blogspot.com.

Patricia L. Stebelton is the author of six published novels. She also has short stories in various compiled books. Patricia and her husband live in a picturesque town in the heart of Michigan. She enjoys family activities and commissioned art projects. Contact her at plstebelton@yahoo.com.

Sylvia Stewart landed in the Belgian Congo as a child. She spent ten years growing up in Africa. She and her husband served the Lord thirty-two years in Malawi and Ethiopia.

Delores E. Topliff lives near Minneapolis, Minnesota. She loves Jesus, family, grandchildren, friends, writing, college teaching, mission trips, travel, and her small farm.

Susan M. Watkins, award-winning author, wrote for *The 700 Club*. She's featured in multiple publications and on CBN.com. Additional credits include work with Gloria Gaynor and Max Lucado.

Agnes Lawless Weaver wrote *The Drift into Deception, Captivated by God,* and *Under His Wings*. She is the coauthor of *Time and Again: God's Sovereignty in the Lives of Two Bible Translators in the Philippines*.

Marie Weaver is a writer of Christian devotionals, stories, and children's books who is also a speaker at various events. See her blog at www.mariesdevotions.wordpress.com.

Joyce Williams is an author and speaker who has also been a pastor's wife and ministry founder. She is the Kansas representative for the Billy Graham Evangelistic Association.

James Stuart Bell is a Christian publishing veteran and the owner of Whitestone Communications, a literary development agency. He is the editor of many story collections, including *Angels, Miracles, and Heavenly Encounters*; *Heaven Touching Earth*; and *Encountering Jesus*, as well as the coauthor of numerous books in the COMPLETE IDIOT'S GUIDE series. He has cover credit on over one hundred books, and he and his wife live in the western suburbs of Chicago.

More True Stories of God's Love and Provision

Compiled by James Stuart Bell

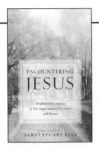

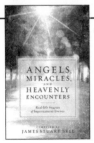
⬦ BETHANYHOUSE

Stay up-to-date on your favorite books and authors with our free e-newsletters. Sign up today at bethanyhouse.com.

Find us on Facebook. facebook.com/BHPnonfiction

Follow us on Twitter. @bethany_house